Table of Contents

Using this Guide ·· ii
Suggested Material ·· ii
Optional Resources ·· iii

Unit 1 – Numbers to 10,000 ·· 1
    Part 1: Thousands, Hundreds, Tens and Ones ······ 2
    Part 2: Number Patterns ······································ 8

Unit 2 – Addition and Subtraction ····························· 12
    Part 1: Sum and Difference ································· 14
    Part 2: Adding Ones, Tens, Hundreds and Thousands ······ 22
    Part 3: Subtracting Ones, Tens, Hundreds and Thousands ······ 27
    Part 4: Two-Step Word Problems ························· 35

Unit 3 – Multiplication and Division ························· 38
    Part 1: Looking Back ··· 40
    Part 2: More Word Problems ····························· 51
    Part 3: Multiplying Ones, Tens, Hundreds and Thousands ······ 60
    Part 4: Quotient and Remainder ························· 70
    Part 5: Dividing Hundreds, Tens and Ones ·········· 77

Review ·· 85

Unit 4 – Multiplication Tables of 6, 7, 8 and 9 ········· 86
    Part 1: Looking Back ··· 88
    Part 2: Multiplying and Dividing by 6 ················· 92
    Part 3: Multiplying and Dividing by 7 ················· 92
    Part 4: Multiplying and Dividing by 8 ················· 104
    Part 5: Multiplying and Dividing by 9 ················· 108

Unit 5 – Money ··· 116
    Part 1: Dollars and Cents ································· 117
    Part 2: Addition ·· 121
    Part 3: Subtraction ·· 124

Review ·· 130

Mental Math Answer Key ·· 131
Textbook Answer Key ··· 133
Workbook Answer Key ··· 140

Using this Guide

This book is a guide for teachers using the *Primary Mathematics* curriculum. It is designed to help teachers understand the course material, see how each section fits in with the curriculum as a whole, and prepare the day's lesson. The course material is divided into 80 sessions. Sessions can be combined for one day's lesson, if necessary to finish the curriculum by then end of the semester, by spending less time on class participation or discussion or not having as many problems for practice during class time.

This guide is designed to be used with both the U.S. edition and the third edition of *Primary Mathematics*. U.S. conventions and spellings are used in this guide, such as using commas for thousands and colons for time, and not using "and" in writing out whole numbers in words. However, any items specific to either edition, such as different answers, different page numbers, and different exercise numbers, are clearly indicated.

This guide includes some worksheets, which can be copied for single class use only.

Workbook exercises can be gone over in class or assigned as homework.

Suggested Material

Number discs
   These are discs with 1, 10, 100, and 1000 written on them. Have some that can be displayed; you can write the numbers on transparent counters if you have an overhead projector, or make some cardboard ones with a sticky or magnetic back. You can also simply draw circles on the board and label them. For student manipulatives, you can write the numbers on opaque counters. Each student or group of students should have 18 of each type. Though discs students can handle can make the lesson more concrete, it can also be time consuming. To save time, students could also draw circles on their place-value chart. If they do so, they do not have to write the 1, 10, or 100 in each circle representing a disc; the column the disc is placed in indicates its value.

Number cards
   You will need various number cards for games or group activities. You can use index cards, but make sure that the number does not show through the card. Many activities will call for four sets of number cards 0-9 for each group. These can be made from playing cards by removing the face cards, making the Ace a 1, and whiting out the 1 and the symbols for the 10's to make them 0's. You can also write the numbers on blank playing cards. Such cards will be easier to handle than index cards.

Number cubes
   This is a cube that can be labeled with different numbers. You need enough for each group of students to have two number cubes.

Place-value chart
   Each student should have a reusable place-value chart with four columns for thousands, hundreds, tens, and ones. They can be made on thin cardboard and placed within a plastic sleeve protector so that students can write on them with dry-erase markers, or lines can be drawn on personal-sized white boards. If you are using number discs the place-value charts should be large enough to place discs on and move them around.

Hundreds board

This is a chart with squares in a 10 x 10 array numbered from 1 to 100. Have one that can be displayed and written on. You will also need to display a blank hundreds board, or a 10 x 10 array but without numbers in the squares. For students, you can use laminated hundreds boards with spaces large enough to be covered up by counters, one for each student, or you can use reproducible paper hundreds boards that students can mark.

Counters

Use the opaque round counters that will fit on a hundreds board, or cubes, or any suitable counter. They should be in 4-5 different colors.

Multilink cubes

These are cubes that can be connected to each other on all 6 sides such as Connect-a-cubes.

Multiplication and division flash cards

Money

Use some dimes and pennies that can be displayed/stuck to the board. You can also simply draw them.

Optional Resources

Extra Practice for Primary Mathematics 3 (U.S. Edition)

This workbook has two to four page exercises covering topics from *Primary Mathematics 3A* and *Primary Mathematics 3B*. The level of difficulty and format of the problems is similar to that of the *Primary Mathematics*. Answers are in the back.

Primary Mathematics Challenging Word Problems 3 (U.S. Edition)

This workbook has word problems only. The problems are topically arranged, with the topics following the same sequence as *Primary Mathematics 3A* and *3B*. Each topic starts with three worked examples, followed by practice problems and then challenge problems. Although the computation skills needed to solve the problems is at the same level as the corresponding *Primary Mathematics*, the problem solving techniques necessary in the challenge section are sometimes more advanced than needed for the problems in the textbook or workbook, and the problems sometimes require more than one step to solve. It is a good source, though, of extra word problems that can be discussed in class or of enrichment problems for more capable students. Answers are in the back.

Primary Mathematics Intensive Practice 3A (U.S. Edition)

This supplemental workbook has one set of problems for each topic in *Primary Mathematics*. Each topical exercise has questions of varying levels of difficulty, but the difficulty level is usually higher than that in the *Primary Mathematics* textbook or workbook. Some of the word problems are quite challenging and require the students to extend their understanding of the concepts and to develop problem solving abilities. Students may not be able to solve all the problems in this section independently even if they have a good understanding of the concepts due to the advanced problem-solving required. There is also a section called "Take the Challenge!" with non-routine problems that can be used to further develop students' problem solving abilities. Answers are located in the back.

Vroot and Vroom CD-ROM

This CD-ROM contains learning activities and two games. Topics covered include material from both Primary Mathematics 3 and 4. The following chart correlates the different activities to the appropriate part of *Primary Mathematics 3A*.

Primary Mathematics 3A		*Vroot and Vroom* *Primary Three*
Anytime		Game 1
Unit 1 – Addition and Subtraction	Part 1 – Sum and Difference	Game 2, Mission 3
Unit 3 – Multiplication and Division	Part 2 – More Word Problems	Problem Solving Learn and Explore Activity 1 Activity 2 Challenge 1
Unit 4 – Multiplication Tables of 6, 7, 8 and 9	Part 2 – Multiplying and Dividing by 9	Game 2, Mission 1

Unit 1 – Numbers to 10,000

Objectives
- Read and write numbers less than 10,000.
- Relate each digit in a 4-digit number to its place value.
- Compare and order numbers within 10,000.

Suggested number of sessions: 6

	Objectives	Textbook	Workbook	Activities
Part 1 : Thousands, Hundreds, Tens and Ones				**4 sessions**
1	▪ Relate 4-digit numbers to thousands, hundreds, tens, and ones. ▪ Read and write 4-digit numbers and corresponding number words.	pp. 6-7 p. 8, tasks 1-2	Ex. 1	1.1a
2	▪ Relate each digit in a 4-digit number to its place value.	p. 9, tasks 3-6	Ex. 2	1.1b
3	▪ Compare and order 4-digit numbers.	pp. 10-11, tasks 7-14	Ex. 3	1.1c
4	▪ Practice.	p. 12, Practice 1A p. 13, Practice 1B		1.1d
Part 2 : Number Patterns				**2 sessions**
5	▪ Count on or back by 1, 10, 100, or 1000. ▪ Recognize number patterns involving counting on or back by ones, tens, hundreds, and/or thousands.	p. 14 pp. 15-16, tasks 1-4	Ex. 4	1.2a
6	▪ Practice.	p. 17, Practice 1C		1.2b

Part 1: Thousands, Hundreds, Tens and Ones (pp. 6-13)   **4 sessions**

Objectives

- Relate 4-digit numbers to thousands, hundreds, tens, and ones.
- Read and write 4-digit numbers.
- Relate each digit in a 4-digit number to its place value.
- Compare and order 4-digit numbers.

Materials

- Base-10 blocks that can be displayed
- Number discs for 1, 10, 100, 1000, and one 10,000 that can be displayed
- Number discs for students
- Opaque bags to hold discs, one for each group
- Place-value charts for students
- Number cubes, labeled 1-6, one per group
- Number cubes labeled with two +1's, two +10's, and two +100's, one per group
- Number cards 0-9, 4 sets per group
- Cards (e.g., 5" by 8" index cards) with 3-digit or 4-digit numbers written on them (mostly 4-digit numbers), one card per student

Homework

- Workbook Exercise 1
- Workbook Exercise 2
- Workbook Exercise 3

Notes

In *Primary Mathematics 2A*, students learned to relate 3-digit numbers to the place value concept and to compare and order 3-digit numbers. This is extended here to 4-digit numbers, and the place value concept is reinforced.

In *Primary Mathematics*, 4-digit numbers are written without the optional comma after the thousands. Number words are written with a comma after the word *thousand* only.

Place-value charts are used extensively in this and the next two units. A place-value chart is a table divided into columns or adjacent "places". You will need to use charts with four columns: thousands, hundred, tens, and ones.

Base-10 materials, such as base-10 blocks, are placed in the appropriate columns. Unit-cubes go in the "Ones" column, ten-rods in the "Tens" column, and hundred-flats in the "Hundreds" column, and a thousand-cube in the "Thousands" column. The number 1136 is represented by 1 thousand-cube in the "Thousands" place or column, 1 hundred-flat in the "Hundreds" place, 3 ten-rods in the "Tens" place, and 6 unit-cubes in the "Ones" place.

Thousands	Hundreds	Tens	
1	1	3	6

Since there are only nine digits in our base-10 system, the highest number of base-10 objects that should remain in any one column on the chart after all operations are completed is 9. If there are 10 or more ones in the "Ones" column, for example when adding 8 and 9, ten of them are "traded in" for a ten and the ten is placed in the tens column or box. This guide uses the term "renamed." Ten ones can be "renamed" as one ten.

Base-10 blocks are a concrete representation of numbers since the student can readily see that a ten-rod is made up of ten ones and a hundred-flat is made up of 10 tens or 100 ones.

In *Primary Mathematics 2A*, students also used number discs as base-ten material. These are discs or circles with 1, 10, 100, or 1000 written on them. They learned that a 10-disc can be replaced with, or renamed as, ten 1-discs, a 100 disc can be renamed as ten 10-discs, and a 1000-disc can be renamed as ten 100-discs. Number discs will be used extensively in *Primary Mathematics*. They are more abstract than base-10 blocks, since the student cannot physically see ten 1-discs in a 10-disc, and the sizes are not proportional. You will find your students completely comfortable with number discs. Not only are they are easier to draw on the board, but being mid-way to abstraction, number discs are helpful to student concentration on number and place value. Further, their use will be easily extended to include decimal places.

Thousands	Hundreds	Tens	Ones
4	1	3	6

You should have plenty of number discs for your class so that all students can use them. Ideally, you need about eighteen of each kind for each student or group of students working together. After initial use of them when first learning a concept, students can then simply draw circles on the place-value chart.

Activity 1.1a   **Four-digit numbers**

1. Review 3-digit numbers and introduce 4-digit numbers using concrete objects.
   - Use base-10 blocks. Display (or draw) a place-value chart with columns for ones, tens, hundreds, and thousands.
     o Count out 9 unit-cubes onto the Ones column. Add one more. Remind the students that only 9 can go into the Ones place. Ask them what they need to do to show ten. In order to show amounts more than 9 with numerals, we need to imagine grouping whatever we are counting into groups of 10. Then we can write the number of groups of ten, and then the ones left over that do not make a whole group of 10. To show the on the place-value chart, we trade in 10 ones for a ten. Replace the ones with a ten-rod and put it on the chart in the Tens column. Tell students you now have one ten in the Tens place. Write the number 10 below the chart, with the 1 under the Tens column and the 0 under the Ones column. Remind your students that the 0 is a place holder, showing that there are no ones. We know whether the digit means groups of tens or just ones by its place in the number.
     o Have the students count by tens as you place 9 more tens on the chart. When you have 10 tens, remind them that we only have 9 digits, so to write a number for an amount with more than 9 tens, we again think of grouping the tens into a ten tens, which is a hundred ones. Replace 10 ten-rods with a hundred-flat and put it on the chart in the Hundreds column. Now write the number 100 under the chart. Ask students what the 1 means, and what each 0 means. (1 means one hundred, 0 means no tens, 0 means no ones)
     o Count out 9 more hundreds. Tell your students that, as with the other places, the hundreds place can only hold 9 hundreds. Replace the ten hundreds with a thousand-cube and write 1000 below the chart. Remind students that this number is one thousand.
   - Use number discs that can be displayed, or draw them on the board.
     o Place a 1-disc on the board along with a unit cube and tell the students that this represents one. Place a 10-disc on the board along with a 10-rod. Remind students that a 10-disc stands for 1 ten, and represents ten ones put together into a group. Ask how many 1-discs are equal to a 10-disc (10). Similarly, equate the 100-disc with a 100-flat and the 1000 disc with a 1000-cube.
     o With the class, count out nine 1000-discs and place them on the place-value chart. Tell them that with one more thousand, another place value is needed. Write 10,000. Tell them this is read as "ten thousand." Write "ten thousand" on the board.
     o Ask them for the number of thousands in ten thousand.
   - Extend the discussion as follows, illustrating when possible with the number discs:

     o How many <u>ones</u> are in 1? (1)
     o How many ones are in 10? (10)
     o How many ones are in 100? (100)
     o How many ones are in 1000? (1000)
     o How many <u>tens</u> are in 10? (1)
     o How many tens are in 100? (10)
     o How many tens are in 1000? (100)
     o How many tens are in 10,000? (1000)
     o How many <u>hundreds</u> are in 100? (1)
     o How many hundreds are in 1000? (10)
     o How many hundreds are in 10000? (100)

- Place four 1000-discs on the chart. To find the number of hundreds, ask how many are in one of these thousands, then in the next thousand, etc. Lead them to see that there are ten in each thousand, and so 10 x 4 in 4 thousands.
    - How many <u>hundreds</u> are in 4000? (40)
    - How many <u>tens</u> are in 4000? (400)
    - How many <u>ones</u> are in 4000? (4000)
- Discuss **textbook p. 6** and the **top of p. 7** with the students.

- Write some additional 3-digit and 4-digit numbers on the board and ask the students to give the number of thousands, hundreds, tens, and ones. Include ones with 0 as a place holder. For example:
    - 436 = 4 hundreds + 3 tens + 6 ones = 400 + 30 + 6
    - 802 = 8 hundreds + 0 tens + 2 ones = 800 + 2
    - 3421 = 3 thousands + 4 hundreds + 2 tens + 1 one
    - 4009 = 4 thousands + 0 hundreds + 0 tens + 9 ones = 4000 + 9

2. Read and write numbers within 10,000.
   - Provide each student with number discs and a place value chart.
     - Write a 4-digit number, such as 8765, on the board, and read it to them. Tell them that sometimes 4-digit numbers are written with a comma before the last 3 digits (after the thousands place). Write the version with a comma on the board. Write 10,000 and tell them that whenever we have 5-digits in the number, we always write a comma before the last 3 digits.
     - Write the number in words and have them copy it.
     - Repeat with other numbers, including some containing 0 as place holder, and have the students illustrate the numbers with number discs. Point out that if there are no hundreds or tens between the thousands place and the ones place, we don't say those places when reading the number.

8765   8,765
eight thousand, seven hundred sixty-five

1630 one thousand, six hundred thirty
4013 four thousand, thirteen
5006 five thousand, six
3100 three thousand, one hundred

3. Discuss **tasks (c)-(e), textbook p. 7**.
   - Have students supply the answers.
   - For (d) and (e) on p. 7, provide some additional practice.
   - Have your students also try counting backwards, for example from 8010 to 7990.

4. Discuss **tasks 1-2, textbook p. 8**.
   - For task 2 on p. 8, have students write the addition expression and number words (e.g. 2000 + 40 + 5 = 2045, two thousand, forty-five).

Workbook Exercise 1

Activity 1.1b   **Place value**

1. Relate each digit in a 4-digit number to its place value.
   - Discuss **tasks 3-6, textbook p. 9**.
   - Provide students with place-value charts and number discs.
     o Write two 4-digit numbers with the same digits but in a different order, such as 1234 and 3124 on the board. Have students illustrate both numbers. Point to the digits and ask what each digit stands for.
     o Ask for the digits in a certain place value. For example, point to 1234 and ask for the digit in the tens place.
     o Ask students for numbers with digits in certain place values. For example, ask for a number that has 3 in the hundreds place.

2. Practice renaming and writing 4-digit numbers and number words.
   - Students can do **problems 1-4, Practice 1A, textbook p. 12**.
   - Write numbers, number words, or addition sentences on the board and have the students place the corresponding number of discs on their charts. For example:
     o 8092
     o 4000 + 100 + 30 + 6
     o Two thousand, sixty-four
   - Dictate some numbers and have students write both the numbers and the number words.
   - Write some numbers as sums of thousands, hundreds, tens, and ones, but out of order, such as 90 + 4 + 2000 + 300, and have your students write the corresponding number and number word (2394; two thousand, three hundred ninety-four).
   - Divide students up into groups. Provide each student with a place-value chart and each group with a bag containing number discs for 1, 10, and 100. There should be a lot of 100-discs. Provide a few additional discs of each kind, plus some 1000-discs.
     o Each student grabs a handful of discs from the bag, places them on their charts, and writes the corresponding number and number word. If the student draws more than 9 of one type of disc, he or she must trade in 10 of them for a disc for the next place.

Workbook Exercise 2

Activity 1.1c   **Compare and order 4-digit numbers**

1. Compare and order numbers within 10,000.
   - Discuss **task 7, textbook p. 10**.
     o Write the numbers being compared above each other with the digits aligned. You can also illustrate the numbers on place-value charts with the discs for one number right above the discs for the other number.
     o Lead students to see that to compare two numbers we first compare the digit in the highest place value. If they are the same, we then compare the digits in the next highest place value, and so on.
   - Write a 4-digit and a 3-digit number on the board, such as 349 and 2458. Lead students to realize that the first number, although it starts with a greater digit than the second, is smaller, because the digit is in the hundreds, rather than the thousands place. Align them vertically, putting a 0 before the first number in the thousands place to emphasize that there are less thousands in the first number.

                                                                    0349

                                                                    2458

2. Have students do **tasks 8-14, textbook pp. 10-11**.
   - As students supply the answers, ask them to explain their answer. For example, in 8(b), 8004 is less than 8040 because 0 tens are less than 4 tens.

3. Provide further practice.
   - Ask the students to arrange the numbers 8332, 7562, 7462, 7458, 8325, and 7457 in order from smallest to greatest.
   - Have them play one of the games below.

4. **Games**:
   - Divide students into groups of four. Each student needs a place-value chart.
     - Game 1 – Provide each group with a number cube labeled with numerals (you can use a regular die, or use a number cube labeled with 4-9 or a different set of six numbers). Students take turns throwing the number cube until each has thrown it four times. After each throw, the player must decide whether to write the number thrown in the thousands place, the hundreds place, the tens place, or the ones place. Once written it must remain in that place. The players do not show each other their numbers until all have written 4 digits. After all have a 4-digit number, the players compare numbers. The highest number wins. Students record all numbers in order for each round.
     - Game 2 – Provide each group with 4 sets of number cards 0-9. Cards are shuffled and placed face down in the middle. Students draw four lines on a piece of paper on which to write the digits and take turns drawing a card. Play proceeds as in game 1.

   - Prepare in advance cards with 3-digit or 4-digit numbers on them. Divide students into teams. Give the team leader enough cards for each member of the team. After all teams have their cards, tell them to begin. The team leader hands a card to each team member. Then the team must line up in order of the numbers on their cards. The first team to line up in order wins.

Workbook Exercise 3

Activity 1.1d   Practice

1. Have students do problems from **Practice 1A, textbook p. 12** and **Practice 1B, textbook p. 13** and discuss their answers.

2. **Game** – Renaming in addition.
   - Divide students into groups. Provide each group with number discs (1's, 10's, 100's, and 1000's) and two number cubes, one labeled 1-6 and one labeled with two $\boxed{+1\text{'s}}$, two $\boxed{+10\text{'s}}$, and two $\boxed{+100\text{'s}}$. Provide each student with a place-value chart.
   - Students take turns throwing both cubes. They collect number discs according to the number on the dice. For example, if they roll a $\boxed{5}$ and $\boxed{+10\text{'s}}$, they collect five 10-discs. Each time they have ten 1-discs, they must trade them in for a 10-disc. If they have ten 10-discs, they trade them in for a 100-disc, and if they have ten 100-discs, they trade them in for a 1000-disc. The first player to have nine 1000-discs (9000) wins.
   - For shorter game time, use a lower target number, such as five 1000-discs.

Part 2: Number Patterns (pp. 14-16)   2 sessions

Objectives

- Add 1, 10, 100, or 1000 to a number within 10,000.
- Subtract 1, 10, 100, or 1000 from a number within 10,000.
- Recognize number patterns which involve counting by 1's, 10's, 100's, or 1000's.

Materials

- Number discs that can be displayed (1's, 10's, 100's, 1000's)
- Number discs for students (1's, 10's, 100's, 1000's)
- Place-value charts for students
- Number cube, one per group
- Number cube labeled with two −1's, two −10's, or two −100's, one per group
- Worksheets with number sequences for groups or individual students (see activity 1.2a below)

Homework

- Workbook Exercise 4

Notes

In this section, the student must focus on the place value of the digit and add to or subtract from that digit.

Activity 1.2a   **Number patterns**

1. Count on or back by 1, 10, 100, or 1000.
   - Draw a place-value chart. Use number discs to place a 4-digit number on the chart. Write the number. Call on students to give the number that is 1 more or 1 less, 10 more or 10 less, 100 more or 100 less, 1000 more or 1000 less than the number on the chart, adding or removing the corresponding number disc and writing the given number. Do numbers where only the digit in one place value is changed. For example:
     - What number is 10 more than the number 4575? (4585)
     - What number is 100 more than 4585? (4685)
     - What number is 1000 more than 4685? (5685)
     - What number is 1 less than 5685? (5684)
     - What number is 100 less than 5684? (5584)
   - Repeat without the number discs and place value chart. Write the equations. For example:
     - 4567 + 100 = ?
     - 8912 – 1000 = ?
   - Repeat with number discs above but do problems where the digit for two or three place values change. Illustrate with a place-value chart and number discs. For example:
     - What is 1 less than 3910? (3909)
     - What is 1 less than 3900? (3899)
     - What number is 10 more than 3899? (3909)
     - What number is 100 more than 3909? (4009)
   - Repeat without number discs. Write the equations.
     - 3298 + 10 = ?
   - Provide students with place-value charts and number discs. Write a 4-digit number on the board. Have student place discs on their charts to illustrate the numbers. Give instructions such as "add 100 to the number. What is the number now?" or "Subtract 1000 from the number. What is the number now?"
   - Write two numbers that differ by 1, 10, 100, or 1000. Ask students to illustrate the first number and then determine what they need to do to get the next number. Write an equation where they must fill in " + " or " – " and the amount being added or removed. For example:
     - 2406 _____ = 2306   →   2406 – 100 = 2306

2. Discuss **textbook p. 14** and **tasks 1-4, textbook pp. 15-16.** In task 4, students need to determine which digit is being increased or decreased.

3. Provide some additional practice.
   - For more practice on number patterns, write number sequence on the board where the tens, hundreds, or thousands increase or decrease by 1. Students extend the pattern or fill in any missing numbers. For example:
     - 4123, 5123, 6123, _____
     - 3932, _____ , 3732, 3632

- Write a starting number and the pattern the sequence should follow on the board. Ask the students to create a sequence 5 terms long following the given description for the pattern. For example:
  - 3091: Increase by 10's
  - 4302: Decrease by 100's

Workbook Exercise 4

Activity 1.2b   **Practice**

1. Have students do problems from **Practice 1C, textbook p. 17** and discuss their answers.

2. Use the worksheet on the next page for additional practice.

3. **Game** – Renaming in subtraction.
   - Divide students into groups. Provide each group with number discs (1's, 10's, 100's, and 1000's) and two number cubes, one labeled with 1-6 and the other with two -1's, two -10's, and two -100's. Provide each student with a place-value chart. Students start with nine 1000-discs.
   - Students take turns rolling both dice. They take away number discs according to the dice. For example, if they roll a 5 and -10's, they take away five 10's. They trade in a 1000 for ten 100-discs, or a 100-disc for ten 10-discs, or a 10-disc for then 1-discs as necessary. The first player to get rid of all his or her number discs wins.
   - To reduce game time, start with fewer 1000-discs.

Mental Math 1

1. $3687 + 1 =$ _____

2. $8952 - 10 =$ _____

3. $8304 - 1 =$ _____

4. $6212 + 100 =$ _____

5. $5731 - 1 =$ _____

6. $8304 - 1 =$ _____

7. $8741 - 1000 =$ _____

8. $9874 - 100 =$ _____

9. $3478 - 10 =$ _____

10. $6587 + 1 =$ _____

11. $3240 + 1000 =$ _____

12. $3820 - 100 =$ _____

13. $9777 - 1 =$ _____

14. $8229 + 10 =$ _____

15. $1234 - 10 =$ _____

16. $8262 - 1000 =$ _____

17. $100 + 1902 =$ _____

18. $1000 + 7864 =$ _____

19. $100 + 5200 =$ _____

20. $10 + 5232 =$ _____

21. $3670 - 1 =$ _____

22. $4702 - 10 =$ _____

23. $3054 - 100 =$ _____

24. $6589 + 1 =$ _____

25. $3491 + 10 =$ _____

26. $2940 - 100 =$ _____

27. $2322 - 10 =$ _____

28. $5400 + 1000 =$ _____

29. $100 + 1902 =$ _____

30. $10 + 1845 =$ _____

31. $10,000 - 1000 =$ _____

32. $3240 + 1001 =$ _____

Unit 2 – Addition and Subtraction

Objectives

- Understand the terms **sum** and **difference**.
- Solve 1-step and 2-step word problems involving addition and subtraction.
- Use the part-whole and comparison models to represent word problems.
- Add numbers up to 10,000.
- Subtract numbers up to 10,000.

Suggested number of sessions: 16

	Objectives	Textbook	Workbook	Activities
Part 1 : Sum and Difference				**5 sessions**
7	▪ Understand the terms **sum** and **difference**. ▪ Draw comparison models to represent mathematical statements.	p. 18 p. 19, tasks 1-2		2.1a
8	▪ Draw part-whole models to represent mathematical statements.	p. 19, task 3	Ex. 5	2.1b
9	▪ Review addition and subtraction of 3-digit numbers.	p. 22, Practice 2A, #1-4 p. 23, Practice 2B, #1-4		2.1c
10	▪ Solve 1-step word problems using pictorial models.	pp. 20-21, tasks 4-7 p. 22, Practice 2A, #5-9 P. 23, Practice 2B, #5-6	Ex. 6	2.1d
11	▪ Solve word problems that take two steps to solve.	p. 21, task 8 p. 23, Practice 2B, #7-9	Ex. 7	2.1e
Part 2 : Adding Ones, Tens, Hundreds and Thousands				**3 sessions**
12	▪ Add ones, tens, or hundreds to a 4-digit number.	p. 25, tasks 1-4		2.2a
13	▪ Add a number within 10,000 to a 4-digit number, with renaming once.	p. 24 p. 26, task 5	Ex. 8	2.2b
	▪ Add a number within 10,000 to a 4-digit number, with renaming twice.	p. 26, tasks 6-7		
14	▪ Add a number, within 10,000 to a 4-digit number with renaming three times.	p. 27, tasks 8-9	Ex. 9	2.2c

	Objectives	Textbook	Workbook	Activities
Part 3 : Subtracting Ones, Tens, Hundreds and Thousands				**6 sessions**
15	• Subtract ones, tens, or hundreds from a 4-digit number.	p. 29, tasks 1-4		2.3a
16	• Subtract a number within 10,000 from a 4-digit number, with renaming once.	p. 28 p. 30, task 5	Ex. 10	2.3b
	• Subtract a number within 10,000 from a 4-digit number, with renaming twice.	p. 30, tasks 6-7		
17	• Subtract a number within 10,000 from a 4-digit number, with renaming three times.	p. 31, tasks 8-9	Ex. 11	2.3c
18	• Subtract a number within 10,000 from a 4-digit number, where renaming occurs over several place values for one step.	pp. 32-33, tasks 10-14	Ex. 12	2.3d
19	• Practice.	p. 34, Practice 2C		2.3e
20	• Subtract from thousands. (Optional)	p. 35, Practice 2D		2.3f
Part 4 : Two-step Word Problems				**2 sessions**
	Objectives	**Textbook**	**Workbook**	**Activities**
21	• Solve simple two-step word problems using pictorial models.	p. 36 p. 37, tasks 1-2	Ex. 13	2.4a
22	• Practice.	p. 38, Practice 2E	Review 1	2.4b

Part 1: Sum and Difference (pp. 18-23)   5 sessions

Objectives

*   Understand the terms **sum** and **difference**.
*   Represent mathematical statements with pictorial models.
*   Use pictorial models to solve one-step addition and subtraction word problems.

Materials

*   Unit cubes or squares that can be displayed
*   Number discs that can be displayed (1's, 10's 100's, 1000's)
*   Number discs for students

Homework

*   Workbook Exercise 5
*   Workbook Exercise 6
*   Workbook Exercise 7

Notes

In *Primary Mathematics* 1 and 2, students learned to relate addition and subtraction to the part-whole concept and to use subtraction to compare two sets of objects using subtraction. However, the terms **sum** and **difference** were not formally used. These terms are introduced here through pictorial models. There are two types of models being introduced here: a part-whole model using one bar, and a comparison model using two or more bars.

Modeling is a tool that can be used to solve problems. The ability to draw models will be useful later in translating word problems into algebraic equations. In algebra, an unknown is represented by a variable, such as x. In modeling, an unknown bar length can be considered similar to a variable, though problems solved using modeling in *Primary Mathematics* 3-6 are often solved somewhat differently than they would be when setting up an algebraic equation. However, a concrete, pictorial foundation will greatly facilitate the understanding of algebraic representations later. Encourage students to draw models so that they become familiar with modeling and can use it to solve problems when necessary, but do not insist that they draw models in the homework if they can easily solve the problem without a model. Some students can visualize the model mentally.

Students will be adding and subtracting numbers of up to 3-digits in this section, using the formal algorithms for addition and subtraction. This can be reviewed. Students learned this algorithm in *Primary Mathematics 2A*.

The word algorithm originally meant the art of calculating by means of nine digits and a zero. It is used here to mean a procedure for solving a mathematical problem in a finite number of steps that frequently involves repetition of an operation. Note: our use of the term "algorithm" in these notes is meant for you only; do not use it with your students.

In the formal algorithm for addition, write the problem in a vertical format where the digits are aligned in columns for each place. Draw a line under the numbers to separate the sum from the numbers being added.

(1)   First add the ones.
  • If the sum is 10 ones or more, rename it as tens and ones.
  • Write the tens (1) above in the tens places, as a reminder is needed that there is a renamed ten.
  • Write the ones down under the line in the ones place (under the column of ones).
(2)   Then add the tens, including any renamed ten.
  • If the sum is 10 tens (100) or more, rename it as hundreds and tens, Write the hundreds above the hundreds place.
  • Write the tens in the tens place under the line.
(3)   Add the hundreds, including any renamed hundreds.
Continue the process until the digits in all the places have been added.

This process can be illustrated with number discs:

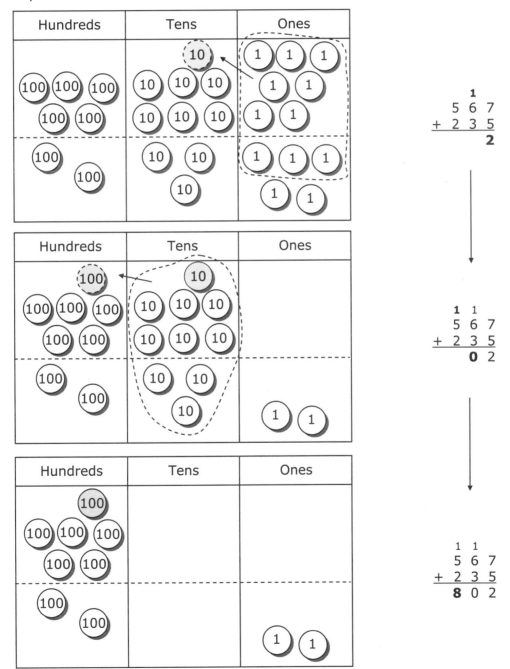

Note: Students may be able to develop other algorithms, such as adding from left to right, but they need to know the formal algorithm.

For the formal algorithm for subtraction:
(1) Try to subtract the ones.
- If there are not enough ones in the top number (the minuend) to subtract from, rename a ten as 10 ones and add them to the ones in the top number.
- There is now one less ten, which can be indicated by crossing out the tens and writing one less ten above them.
- Subtract the ones and write the difference under the line in the ones place.
(2) Then, try to subtract the tens.
- If there are not enough tens in the top number to subtract from, rename a hundred as 10 tens and add them to the tens in the top number. There is now one less hundred.
- Subtract the tens and write the difference written under the line in the tens place.
Continue this process for each place value.

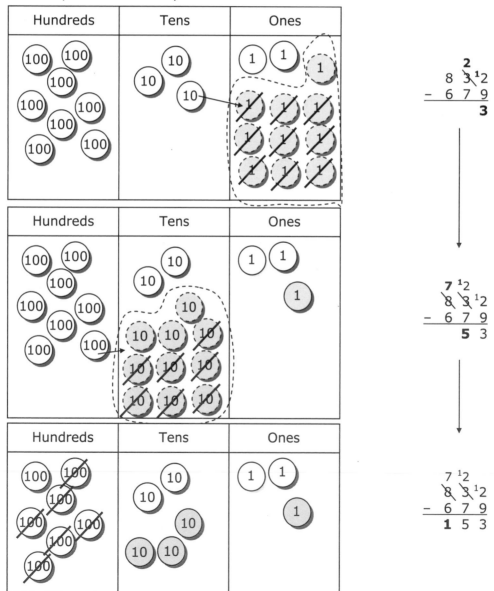

Activity 2.1a   **Sum and difference**

1. Explain the terms sum and difference using concrete objects and comparison bar models.
   - Write the equation 3 + 5 = ? on the board.

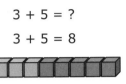

3 + 5 = ?

3 + 5 = 8

   - o Ask for the answer and write it. Explain that when we add two numbers, we are finding their **sum**. The **sum** of 3 and 5 is 8.
   - o Show the 2 parts, using two colors of blocks. Point out each part and the whole. One color shows one part, the other color shows the other part, and both of them together show the whole.
   - Set up the sum again with blocks, and then move one set of blocks down below the other.
     - o Ask your students how many more blocks there are of one color than of the other.
     - o Tell them that we are finding the **difference** between two numbers. To find the difference, we subtract. Write the equation.

5 – 3 = 2

   - Now, show the students how we can draw the two numbers using bars.
     - o Draw the bar for 5, and then ask whether the bar for 3 should be shorter or longer. Draw it below the bar for 5. Point out that for easier comparison we line the bars up, usually on the left.
     - o Draw arrows to label each bar, and write the value of each.
     - o If we are asked to find the **difference**, we can draw an arrow indicating the difference, and label that with a question mark.

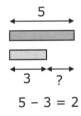

5 – 3 = 2

     - o If we are asked to find the **sum**, we can show that by drawing a bracket at the right and labeling it with a question mark.
     - o Tell the students that what we did is called *modeling the problem* and did it with what is called a **comparison model**. It shows the comparison between the two numbers.

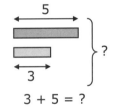

3 + 5 = ?

   - Ask for the **sum** and **difference** of another pair of two digit numbers, such as 14 and 5. Ask them to model the problem. Have them decide how long they should draw the bars on their page and about how much longer one bar should be than the other.

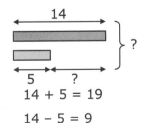

14 + 5 = 19

14 – 5 = 9

   - Then ask them to model some larger two digit numbers, such as 60 and 34, on the same page. They should realize that this second drawing does not have to relate to the first drawing since it is a separate problem. The bar for 60 does not have to be drawn longer than the bar for 14 of the previous problem. It just has to be longer than the bar for 34 in the current problem.

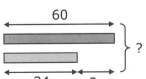

60 + 34 = 94

60 – 34 = 26

2. Discuss **textbook p. 18** and **tasks 1-2, textbook p. 19**.

3. Provide some additional problems, if time permits.
   - Use numbers less than 100. Students should draw reasonable relative lengths for the two numbers. You can draw some models that are obviously unreasonable and guide them in understanding why those are not good representations of the problem.

Activity 2.1b   **Bar models**

1. Draw part-whole pictorial models.

   - Draw a number bond, such as one for 3, 5, and 8.
     - o Remind the students that this shows two parts and a whole. Erase the whole and write the equation.
     - o Ask students what we call the whole. It is the **sum** of the two parts.

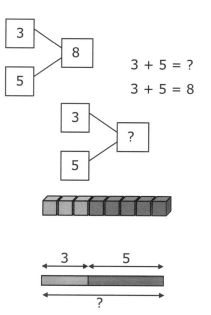

     - o Show blocks of two colors as in Activity 2.1a.
     - o Remind students that we modeled this before by showing one number-part on top of the other, in a comparison model. Tell them that they can also model it by showing one part next to the other.
     - o Draw the part-whole model.
     - o Point out that we draw the larger number longer than the smaller number and label the parts with an arrow or bracket.
     - o Ask them how we could show the whole. Label the entire length of the bar. Since we want to find the whole, we label that with a question mark.
     - o Tell them this is called a **part-whole model**.

   - Draw the number bond again, this time with one of the parts replaced with "?".
     - o Ask students how we find the missing part. We subtract. Write the equation.
     - o Tell students that we can still call the answer the difference. That is, when we are finding the missing part in this number bond, we are also finding the difference between 8 and 3.
     - o Show students how to draw the model. We can draw a bar for the whole, and then draw a line to cut the bar into two parts. We label the whole and one of the parts with the values we know, and the other part with a question mark to show what we want to find.

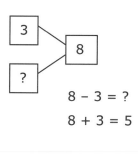

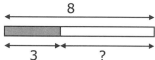

2. Refer to **task 3, textbook p. 19**. Have the students draw models for these.

    • In (a), we are given two parts and asked for a whole, so we could draw a part-whole model. In (b), we are given the whole (the sum) and one part, and asked to find the other part, so we could also draw a part-whole model. In (c) and (d) we are asked to compare the numbers, so we draw comparison models.

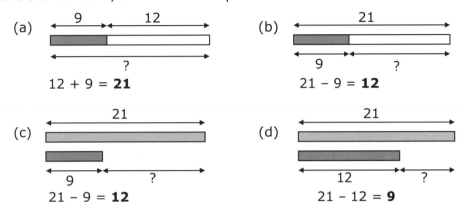

(a)   12 + 9 = **21**

(b)   21 – 9 = **12**

(c)   21 – 9 = **12**

(d)   21 – 12 = **9**

3. Review and practice.

    • Tell your students that drawing models will help them to decide whether they need to add or subtract to solve a problem. Give students some problems to illustrate this and ask them to draw a model and then write the equation. Either a part-whole or a comparison model can be used. Use numbers within 100. For example:

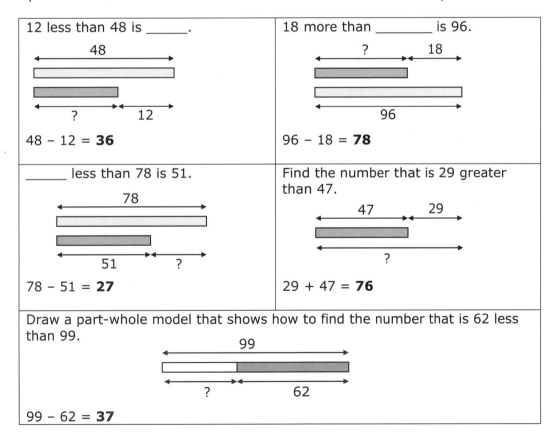

12 less than 48 is _____. 48 – 12 = **36**	18 more than _____ is 96. 96 – 18 = **78**
_____ less than 78 is 51. 78 – 51 = **27**	Find the number that is 29 greater than 47. 29 + 47 = **76**
Draw a part-whole model that shows how to find the number that is 62 less than 99. 99 – 62 = **37**	

Workbook Exercise 5

Activity 2.1c   **Addition and subtraction review**

1. Review addition and subtraction of 2-digit and 3-digit numbers.

   - Review the addition algorithm for numbers of up to 3 digits. If you feel your class needs to start with easier problems, you can start with two-digit numbers and then move on to 3-digit numbers. Do problems where:
     o The ones have to be renamed.
     o The tens have to be renamed.
     o Both the tens and the ones are renamed.
     Illustrate the steps with number discs, as outlined in the notes in this guide.

   - Review the subtraction algorithm with numbers of up to 3 digits. You can start with 2-digit numbers and then move on to 3-digit numbers. Do problems where:
     o The tens have to be renamed.
     o The hundreds have to be renamed.
     o Both the tens and the hundreds have to be renamed.
     o Both hundreds and tens need to be renamed in one step.
     Illustrate the steps with number discs.

   - If your class is weak in addition or subtraction, you may want spend several days on this, and use *Primary Mathematics 2A* for more problems and examples.

2. Have students do **problems 1-4, Practice 2A, textbook p. 22** and **problems 1-4, Practice 2B, textbook p. 23**.

$$\begin{array}{r} \scriptstyle 1 \\ 4\ 6\ 4 \\ +\ 1\ 1\ 9 \\ \hline 5\ 8\ 3 \end{array}$$

$$\begin{array}{r} \scriptstyle 1 \\ 4\ 6\ 4 \\ +\ 1\ 7\ 1 \\ \hline 6\ 3\ 5 \end{array}$$

$$\begin{array}{r} \scriptstyle 1\ \ 1 \\ 4\ 6\ 4 \\ +\ 1\ 7\ 9 \\ \hline 6\ 4\ 3 \end{array}$$

$$\begin{array}{r} \scriptstyle 4 \\ 4\ \cancel{5}\ {}^1 2 \\ -\ 1\ 2\ 8 \\ \hline 3\ 2\ 4 \end{array}$$

$$\begin{array}{r} \scriptstyle 3 \\ \cancel{4}\ {}^1 5\ 2 \\ -\ 1\ 7\ 1 \\ \hline 2\ 8\ 1 \end{array}$$

$$\begin{array}{r} \scriptstyle 3\ \ {}^14 \\ \cancel{4}\ \cancel{5}\ {}^1 2 \\ -\ 1\ 7\ 8 \\ \hline 2\ 7\ 4 \end{array}$$

$$\begin{array}{r} \scriptstyle 3\ \ 9 \\ \cancel{4}\ {}^1\cancel{0}\ {}^1 0 \\ -\ 1\ 7\ 8 \\ \hline 2\ 2\ 2 \end{array}$$

3. Give the students two 3-digit numbers and ask them to model them using the comparison model. Help them determine reasonable relative lengths for the bars. Then ask them to find their sum and their difference.

Activity 2.1d   **Word problems**

1. Use pictorial models to solve one-step word problems involving addition and subtraction.
   - Discuss **tasks 4-7, textbook pp. 20-21**. Ask your students pertinent questions so that they look at each bit of information given in the problem, such as:
     o What do we need to find?
     o What information are we given?
     o Are we given a total? What part is given?
     o Are we given two parts? Which part is larger?
     o Are we comparing two amounts? What two? Which is larger?
   - As you get answers to the problem, illustrate drawing the diagrams step-by-step on the board. For example, in task 4, once the students determine that we are given a total, draw a bar to represent the total. Ask them for the amount and label it. When they determine that we are given one part and find the other, divide up the total bar appropriately. The part we know is less than half of the total bar. Label the parts with

the amount for a known part and a question mark for the unknown amount. Drawing the model step-by-step as they go through the thinking process is a more valuable exercise than simply looking at the finished model in the book. You can call on a student to come to the board and draw the model as the problem is discussed.

2. Provide additional problems.
    *   Make up some problems to write on the board.

        Paul gave $134 to John and had $56 left. How much money did Paul have at first?

        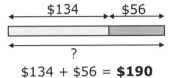

        $134 + $56 = **$190**

    *   Have students work individually on **problems 5-9 Practice 2A, textbook p. 22,** and **problems 5-6 Practice 2B, textbook p. 23**.
    *   After students are finished, call on individual students to draw models and explain their solutions. Discuss alternative models other students may have drawn.

Workbook Exercise 6

Activity 2.1e   **More word problems**

1. Solve word problems with two given steps.
    *   Discuss **task 8, textbook p. 21**. This problem is an introduction to two-step word problems, which will be taught in topic 4 of this unit. The solution to (b) can be found from the given model, but the model can also be redrawn as a part-whole model to show the total if necessary.
    *   Discuss **problems 7-9, Practice 2B, textbook p. 23**, plus any problems not done in the previous activity. Give students time to work on the problems individually, and then call on students to present solutions. Different students may come up with different models.
    *   Discuss additional problems or provide problems for students to work on independently. For example:

        Mary had 120 more beads than Jill. Jill had 68 beads.
        Step 1: How many beads did Mary have?
          68 + 120 = 188
        Mary had 188 beads.
        Step 2: How many beads did the two girls have altogether?
          188 + 68 = 256
        They had 256 beads.

        Daniel and Peter have 450 marbles. Daniel has 248 marbles.
        Step 1: How many marbles does Peter have?
          450 – 248 = 202
        Peter has 202 marbles.
        Step 2: Who has more marbles? How much more?
          248 – 202 = 46
        Daniel has 46 more marbles.

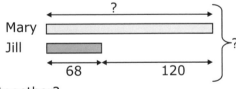

Workbook Exercise 7

Part 2: Adding Ones, Tens, Hundreds and Thousands (pp. 24-27)   3 sessions

Objectives

•   Add numbers within 10,000.

Materials

•   Number discs that can be displayed (1's, 10's, 100's, 1000's)
•   Number discs for students
•   Place-value charts for students
•   Number cards 0-9, four sets per group

Homework

•   Workbook Exercise 8
•   Workbook Exercise 9

Notes

In *Primary Mathematics 2A*, students learned how to add numbers under 1000 with renaming, using the standard algorithm. This concept is extended in this section to numbers under 10,000. Students should be familiar with the procedure with 3-digit numbers and may not have much difficulty in extending it here. Illustrate as many problems as necessary, one step at a time, with number discs, writing each step down as you proceed so that the student sees the connection between the concrete manipulatives and the numerical representation of each step. Allow your student access to the base-10 material when doing the problems. A general procedure is given here.

Write the problem and place the discs on the place value chart. Discuss each step. Ask students to do the calculations.

Step 1: Add the ones.
•   *7 ones + 5 ones = 12 ones = 1 ten 2 ones.*
•   On the chart, trade in 10 ones for 1 ten and place it in the column for tens.
•   On the written problem, write a 1 above the tens and a 2 for the total ones below the line in the ones place.

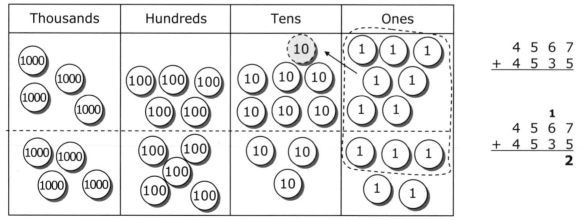

7 ones + 5 ones = 12 ones = 1 ten 2 ones

Step 2: Add the tens.
- Write *6 tens + 3 tens + 1 ten = 10 tens = 1 hundred*.
- On the chart, trade in 10 tens for 1 hundred and place it in the column for hundreds.
- On the written problem, write a 1 above the hundreds and a 0 for the total tens below the line in the tens place.

Thousands	Hundreds	Tens	Ones

6 tens + 3 tens + 1 ten = 10 tens = 1 hundred

Step 3: Add the hundreds.
- Write *5 hundreds + 5 hundreds + 1 hundred = 11 hundreds = 1 thousand 1 hundred*.
- On the chart, trade in 10 hundreds for 1 thousand and place it in the column for thousands.
- On the written problem, write a 1 above the thousands and a 1 for the total hundreds below the line in the tens place.

Thousands	Hundreds	Tens	Ones

5 hundreds + 5 hundreds + 1 hundred = 11 hundreds = 1 thousand 1 hundred

Step 4: Add the thousands.
- On the written problem, write a 9 below the line in the thousands place.

Thousands	Hundreds	Tens	Ones

Activity 2.2a   **Add ones, tens, or hundreds**

1. Add ones, tens, and hundreds.
   - Discuss **task 1, textbook p. 25**.
     - In these problems, no renaming is necessary. Students who have done *Primary Mathematics* previously should be able to keep track of the place value of each digit without seeing them aligned in a vertical format and solve them mentally. They can rewrite them vertically as a check.
     - In (a), add ones to ones, in (b) add tens to tens, in (c) add hundreds to hundreds, and in (d) add thousands to thousands.
     - In (e), the steps for (a), (b), and (c) are combined.
     - In (f), the steps for (a)-(d) are combined.
   - Refer to **tasks 2-4, textbook p. 25**.
     - Illustrate the steps with number discs. In each case, renaming occurs.
     - In task 2, have students add ones and then rename the sum in terms of tens and ones. Repeat with tasks 3 and 4:
       - 8 ones + 2 ones = 10 ones = 1 ten
       - 4 tens + 6 tens = 10 tens = 1 hundred
       - 7 hundreds + 3 hundreds = 10 hundreds = 1 thousand
     - Some students will be able to solve these without rewriting the problem vertically, starting from the left. Allow students to solve whichever addition problems they can mentally but do not require it.

2. **Game**:
   - Divide students into groups. Provide each group with 4 sets of number cards 0-9.
   - Students write down 0 as their starting number. They take turns drawing cards. Three cards are drawn in each round. The first card they draw is ones, the second tens, and the third hundreds. They record the addition sentence, adding the ones, tens, or hundreds to their previous number. For example, in the first round, 4, 8, and 5 are drawn. In the second round, 3, 4 and 6 are drawn. The addition equations for the second round should read: 584 + 3 = 587
                                                 587 + 40 = 627
                                                 627 + 600 = 1227
   - The first player to reach 9000 (or some other target number) in a round wins.
   - Students having difficulty with the additions can use number discs and a place-value chart.

3. Students who are more capable in mental math can do the worksheet on the next page.
   - You may want to discuss methods to mentally add to a single place value. For example, 4689 + 30 can be solved as follows. If you see some students becoming confused in discussion of this short-cut, stop. It is always more important for them to solve problems correctly than to solve them quickly.
     - Looking ahead, adding tens will change the hundreds, but not the thousands. Write down the thousands: **4**
     - Before writing down the hundreds, look ahead to the tens. Adding tens will create another hundred. Write down the hundreds plus one: **47**.
     - Before adding tens, look ahead to the ones. Adding ones won't make another ten. Determine the ten that will result from adding the tens. It is 1 (8 + 3 = 11). Write down 1 for tens: **471**.
     - Add the ones and write down the ones: **4719**.

Mental Math 2

1. 38 + 6 = _____

2. 380 + 60 = _____

3. 3800 + 600 = _____

4. 1246 + 5 = _____

5. 2460 + 50 = _____

6. 4600 + 500 = _____

7. 4601 + 500 = _____

8. 4621 + 500 = _____

9. 1499 + 1 = _____

10. 1499 + 2 = _____

11. 1990 + 10 = _____

12. 1990 + 30 = _____

13. 1999 + 30 = _____

14. 8 + 122 = _____

15. 4 + 69 = _____

16. 51 + 90 = _____

17. 780 + 700 = _____

18. 3430 + 20 = _____

19. 3448 + 9 = _____

20. 2700 + 800 = _____

21. 322 + 80 = _____

22. 922 + 80 = _____

23. 932 + 80 = _____

24. 30 + 767 = _____

25. 8251 + 90 = _____

26. 8951 + 90 = _____

27. 9109 + 6 = _____

28. 9109 + 60 = _____

29. 1227 + 800 = _____

30. 9999 +1 = _____

Activity 2.2b   **Rename once or twice**

1. Add 3-digit or 4-digit numbers where renaming occurs once.
    *   Discuss the example on **textbook p. 24**. Have students set up the problem with their number discs and follow the steps as you illustrate them.
    *   Have the students solve the problems in **task 5, textbook p. 26**. Students should rewrite the problems vertically, aligning the digits. They can turn lined paper sideways and use the columns between the lines to help them align the digits. Illustrate the steps with number discs if necessary.
        *   Tasks 5 (a) and (b) have renaming in the ones.
        *   Tasks 5 (c) and (d) have renaming in the tens.
        *   Tasks 5 (e) and (f) have renaming in the hundreds.

2. Add 3-digit or 4-digit numbers where renaming occurs twice.
    *   Step through the problem in **task 6, textbook p. 26**, where renaming occurs twice. Have students set up the problem with their number discs and follow the steps as you illustrate them.
    *   Have the students solve the problems in **task 7, textbook p. 26**. They should rewrite the problems vertically, aligning the digits.
        *   Task 7 (a) and (b) have renaming in the ones and tens.
        *   Task 7 (c) and (d) have renaming in the tens and hundreds.
        *   Tasks 7 (e) and (f) have renaming in the ones and hundreds.

3. Provide additional practice.
    *   Provide additional practice in addition of numbers within 10,000 with renaming once or twice. You can give students or groups about five problems and have them compete for speed and accuracy in this and later activities.

Workbook Exercise 8

Activity 2.2c   **Rename three times**

1. Add 3-digit or 4-digit numbers where renaming occurs three times.
    *   Step through the problem in **task 8, textbook p. 27**, where renaming occurs three times. Have students set up the problem with their number discs and follow the steps as you illustrate them.
    *   Have the students solve the problems in **task 9, textbook p. 27**. They should rewrite the problems vertically, aligning the digits. Illustrate the steps with number discs if necessary.

2. **Game**:
    *   Divide students into groups. Provide each group with four sets of number cards 0-9, shuffled.
    *   The dealer deals 8 cards to each player. Players must arrange the cards into two 4-digit numbers such that the sum gives the *smallest* number. The player with the smallest numbers wins the point for that round.
    *   After a couple of rounds, ask students to explain how they formed two 4-digit numbers to get the lowest sum. Continue the game once they understand how to form the numbers. The smallest digits should be given the highest place values.

Workbook Exercise 9

| Part 3: Subtracting Ones, Tens, Hundreds and Thousands (pp. 28-35) | 6 sessions |

Objectives

- Subtract numbers within 10,000.

Materials

- Number discs that can be displayed (1's, 10's, 100's, 1000's)
- Number discs for students
- Place-value charts for students
- Number cards 0-9, four sets per group; extra cards for 0, ten per group

Homework

- Workbook Exercise 10
- Workbook Exercise 11
- Workbook Exercise 12

Notes

In *Primary Mathematics 2A*, students learned how to subtract numbers under 1000 with renaming, using the standard algorithm. This concept is extended in this section to numbers under 10,000. The students may be familiar enough with the procedure from 3-digit numbers and may not have much difficulty in extending it here. Illustrate as many problems as necessary, one step at a time, with number discs, writing each step down as you proceed so that the student sees the connection between the concrete manipulatives and the numerical representation of each step. Allow your student to have access to the manipulatives when doing the problems. A general procedure is given here.

Write the problem and place the discs for the first number on the chart. Explain each step and ask students to do the calculations.

Step 1: Subtract the ones.
- There are not enough ones to take away 9 ones. Rename a ten for 10 ones.
- On the chart, trade in 1 hundred for 10 ones and put them in the columns for ones. Write *3 tens 2 ones = 2 tens 12 ones.*
- On the written problem, cross out the 3 tens and write a 2 above it. Write a little 1 in front of the 2 ones to show that there are now 12 ones.
- Remove 9 ones from the chart.
- On the written equation write the difference for the ones below the line.

3 tens 2 ones = 2 tens 12 ones

Step 2: Subtract the tens.
• There are not enough tens to take away 7 tens, so rename a hundred as 10 tens.
• On the chart trade in a hundred for 10 tens and put them in the column for tens. Write *1 hundred 2 tens = 12 tens*. On the written equation, cross out the hundred, write 0 above it, and write a little 1 next to the 2 above the tens.
• Remove 7 tens from the chart. On the written equation, write the difference for the tens below the line in the tens place.

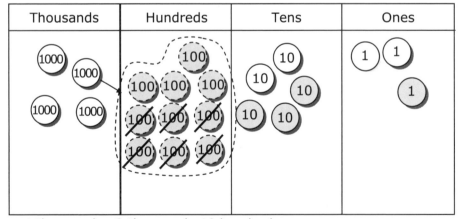

Thousands	Hundreds	Tens	Ones

1 hundred 2 tens = 12 tens

Step 3: Subtract the hundreds.
• There are not enough hundreds, so a thousand must be renamed.
• On the chart trade in a thousand for 10 hundreds and put them in the column for hundreds. Write *4 thousands = 3 thousands 10 hundreds*. On the written equation, cross out the thousand, write 4 above it, and write a little 1 next to the 0 above the hundreds.
• Remove 6 hundreds from the chart. On the written equation, write the difference for the hundreds below the line in the tens place.

Thousands	Hundreds	Tens	Ones

4 thousand = 3 thousands 10 hundreds

Step 4: Subtract the thousands.

Thousands	Hundreds	Tens	Ones

Activity 2.3a   **Subtract ones, tens, and hundreds**

1. Subtract ones, tens, and hundreds.
   - Discuss **task 1, textbook p. 29**.
     - o   In these problems, no renaming is necessary.
     - o   Students should be able to solve these mentally. They can rewrite the problem vertically as a check.
     - o   In (a), ones are subtracted.
     - o   In (b), tens are subtracted.
     - o   In (c), hundreds are subtracted.
     - o   In (d) thousands are subtracted.
     - o   In (e), the steps for (a), (b), and (c) are combined.
     - o   In (f), the steps for (a)-(d) are combined.
   - Discuss **tasks 2-4, text p. 29**.
     - o   Illustrate the steps with number discs on the board.
     - o   In each case, renaming occurs. Rewrite the renaming in terms of place value:
       - ▪   4 tens = 3 tens 10 ones
       - ▪   5 hundreds = 4 hundreds 10 tens
       - ▪   7 thousands = 6 thousands 10 hundreds

2. **Game**:
   - Divide students into groups. Provide each group with number discs and 4 sets of number cards 0-9.
   - Students begin with 9 thousands, 5 hundreds, 5 tens, and 5 ones. They take turns drawing cards. Three cards are drawn in each round. The first card they draw is ones, the second tens, and the third hundreds. Each time they draw a card, they remove the corresponding number of ones, tens, or hundreds, renaming as necessary. They record the subtraction sentence, subtracting the ones, tens, or hundreds from their previous number. For example, in the first round, 4, 8, and 5 are drawn. The equations for the second round should read:
     $$5555 - 4 = 5551$$
     $$5551 - 80 = 5471$$
     $$5471 - 500 = 4971$$
   - The first player to have less than 1000 left wins.

3. Students who are more capable in mental math can do the worksheet on the next page.
   - You can discuss strategies with them. For example, 4619 – 30 can be solved as follows:
     - o   Look at the thousands place of both numbers. No thousands are being subtracted. Look ahead to the hundreds. No hundreds are being subtracted either. Write down the thousands: **4**.
     - o   Before writing down the hundreds, look ahead to the tens. Subtracting tens will require a hundred to be renamed (or subtracting from the hundred). Write down one less hundred: 4**5**.
     - o   Before subtracting tens, look ahead to the ones. Subtracting ones won't require a ten. Determine the tens that will result from subtracting tens, either from having subtracted from the hundred (leaving 7 tens which are added to the ten already there) or from recalling the subtraction fact 11 – 3 = 8. Write down the tens: 45**8**.
     - o   Subtract the ones: 458**9**.
     - o   Or, students can count backwards from 61 tens.

Mental Math 3

1. $59 - 4 =$ _____

2. $590 - 40 =$ _____

3. $5900 - 400 =$ _____

4. $71 - 9 =$ _____

5. $710 - 90 =$ _____

6. $7100 - 900 =$ _____

7. $471 - 9 =$ _____

8. $4710 - 90 =$ _____

9. $4712 - 90 =$ _____

10. $3471 - 9 =$ _____

11. $134 - 8 =$ _____

12. $2510 - 60 =$ _____

13. $1992 - 5 =$ _____

14. $1992 - 500 =$ _____

15. $2518 - 60 =$ _____

16. $100 - 7 =$ _____

17. $2100 - 7 =$ _____

18. $100 - 70 =$ _____

19. $2100 - 70 =$ _____

20. $140 - 60 =$ _____

21. $3410 - 40 =$ _____

22. $653 - 5 =$ _____

23. $1334 - 80 =$ _____

24. $91 - 30 =$ _____

25. $920 - 80 =$ _____

26. $61 - 7 =$ _____

27. $920 - 40 =$ _____

28. $30 - 4 =$ _____

29. $450 - 8 =$ _____

30. $4500 - 8 =$ _____

Activity 2.3b   **Rename once or twice**

1. Subtract 3-digit or 4-digit numbers where renaming occurs once.
    - Discuss the example on **textbook p. 28**. Have students set up the problem with number discs on their place-value charts discs and follow the steps as you illustrate them.
    - Have the students solve the problems in **task 5 textbook, p. 30**. They should rewrite the problems vertically, aligning the digits. Illustrate the steps with number discs if necessary.
        o   In (a) and (b) tens must be renamed
        o   In (c) and (d) hundreds must be renamed
        o   In (e) and (f) thousands must be renamed.
    - Provide additional practice in addition of numbers within 10,000 with renaming once. You can give students or groups around five problems and have them compete for speed and accuracy.

2. Subtract 3-digit or 4-digit numbers where renaming occurs twice.
    - Step through the problem in **task 6, textbook p. 30**, where renaming occurs twice. Have students set up the problem with their number discs and follow the steps as you illustrate them.
    - Have the students solve the problems in **task 7, textbook p. 30**. They should rewrite the problems vertically, aligning the digits.
        o   In (a) and (b) tens and hundreds must be renamed.
        o   In (c) and (d) hundreds and thousands must be renamed.
        o   In (e) and (f) tens and thousands must be renamed.

Workbook Exercise 10

Activity 2.3c   **Rename three times**

1. Subtract three or four digit numbers where renaming occurs three times.
    - Step through the problem in **task 8, textbook p. 31**, where renaming occurs three times. Have students set up the problem with their number discs and follow the steps as you illustrate them.
    - Have the students solve the problems in **task 9, textbook p. 31**. They should rewrite the problems vertically, aligning the digits. Illustrate the steps with number discs if necessary.

2. Game.
    - Divide students into groups. Provide each group with four sets of number cards 1-9, shuffled.
    - The dealer deals 8 cards to each player. Players must arrange the cards into two 4-digit numbers so that the difference gives the smallest number. The player with the smallest difference wins the point for that round.
    - Optional: After a couple of rounds, ask students to explain how they can form two numbers to get the smallest difference. Write 4 digits on the board and challenge students to arrange them into two numbers that give the smallest difference. Extend the discussion to 6 digits and two 3-digit numbers, then 8 digits and two 4-digit numbers.

Workbook Exercise 11

Activity 2.3d   **Rename over several places**

1. Subtract 3-digit or 4-digit numbers where renaming occurs over several place values.
   • Step through the problems in **tasks 10-11, textbook p. 32,** and **task 13, textbook p. 33.** Have students set up the problem with their number discs and follow the steps as you illustrate them.
   • Have the students solve the problems in **task 12, textbook p. 32,** and **task 14, textbook p. 33.** They should rewrite the problems vertically, aligning the digits. Illustrate the steps with number discs if necessary.

2. **Game.**
   • Divide students into groups. Provide each group with three sets of number cards 1-9 and 10 extra 0's, shuffled.
   • The dealer deals 8 cards to each player. Players must arrange the cards into two 4-digit numbers so that the difference gives the smallest number. The player with the smallest difference wins the point for that round.

Workbook Exercise 12

Activity 2.3e   **Practice**

1. Review drawing part-whole and comparison models with problems that involve 4-digit numbers, such as the following:
   ○ What is the number that is 1492 greater than 16 hundreds?
   ○ 361 more than _____ is 4500.
   ○ The difference between the greatest and the smallest of the three numbers 3469, 2301, and 6914 is _____
   ○ What number is 1529 less than 4592?

2. Have students do the problems in **Practice 2C, textbook p. 34.**
   • After students have worked independently on some of the problems, have some of them explain their solutions to the class. Discuss any alternate solutions. Assign any problems not done in class as homework.

Activity 2.3f   **Subtract from one thousand**

1. Have students do the problems in **Practice 2D, textbook p. 35.**
   • After students have worked independently on some of the problems, have some of them explain their solutions to the class. Discuss any alternate solutions. Assign any problems not done in class as homework.

2. Discuss methods for subtracting from thousands mentally.
   • Subtracting from a thousand will be a useful skill for unit 5 and for problems involving adding and subtracting in compound units in *Primary Mathematics 3B.*
   • Display a 1000-disc on a place-value chart.
     ○ Ask students how we can subtract a one from this. Show how the thousand has to be renamed as 9 hundreds, 9 tens, and 10 ones. $1000 = 900 + 90 + 10$

- o A number can be subtracted from 1000 by thinking of it as 9 hundreds, 9 tens, and 10 ones and subtracting first the hundreds, then the tens, and then the ones.

- • Write 1000 – 462 on the board and show how we can do this problem by thinking of 1000 as 9 hundreds, 9 tens, and 10 ones.
  - o Find the difference between 4 and 9 and write that down for 100's: **5.**
  - o Find the difference between 3 and 9 and write that down for 10's: 5**3.**
  - o Find the difference between 2 and 10 and write that down for 1's: 53**8.**

  1000 – 462 = 538

```
  1  0  0  0
 -    4  6  2

     9  9  10
 -   4  6  2
     5  3  8
```

- • Write 1000 – 460 on the board.
  - o In this case, where there are no ones, we think of the 1000 as 9 hundreds and 10 tens. We find the difference between 4 and 9 for hundreds, and 6 and 10 for tens.

```
  1  0  0  0
 -    4  6  0

     9  10 0
 -   4  6  0
     5  4  0
```

- • Write 1000 – 400 on the board.
  - o In this case, where there are no tens or ones, we just find the difference between 4 and 10 for the hundreds.

```
  1  0  0  0
 -    4  0  0
     6  0  0
```

- • To mentally subtract a 3-digit number from 1000, we start at the hundreds and subtract the digits from 9 until the last non-zero digit, which we subtract from a 10.
- • Write some 3-digit numbers on the board and ask students for the difference with 1000.

- • Write 1000 – 34 on the board.
  - o A 2-digit number can be thought of as having a 0 in the hundreds place. So we rename 1000 as 9 hundreds, 9 tens, and 10 ones.
    - ▪ Find the difference between 0 and 9 and write that down for 100's: **9.**
    - ▪ Find the difference between 3 and 9 and write that down for 10's: 9**6.**
    - ▪ Find the difference between 4 and 10 and write that down for 1's: 96**6.**

    1000 – 34 = 966

```
  1  0  0  0
 -       3  4

     9  9  10
 -   0  3  4
     9  6  6
```

- • Try having the students do some problems involving subtraction from a multiple of 1000, such as 3000 – 412. This can be solved mentally by thinking of it as 2000 + 1000 – 412. Find 1000 – 412 mentally, and then add one less thousand.

  3000 – 412
  - o Write down one less thousand for the 1000's: **2.**
  - o Find the difference between 4 and 9 and write that down for the 100's: 2**5.**
  - o Find the difference between 1 and 9 and write that down for the 10's: 25**8.**
  - o Find the difference between 2 and 10 and write that down for the 1's: 258**8.**

  3000 – 412 = 2588
- • Provide students with additional practice. You can use the mental math worksheet on the next page.
- • Game: Divide students into groups and provide each group with four sets of number cards 0-9. The dealer deals out 3 cards face down to all players. Players turn over the cards at the same time and find the difference with 1000. The student who has the lowest or highest number or gets the answer first wins.

Mental Math 4

1. 1000 – 1 = _____

2. 1000 – 10 = _____

3. 1000 – 90 = _____

4. 1000 – 100 = _____

5. 1000 – 900 = _____

6. 1000 – 99 = _____

7. 1000 – 123 = _____

8. 1000 – 456 = _____

9. 1000 – 789 = _____

10. 1000 – 240 = _____

11. 1000 – 241 = _____

12. 1000 – 41 = _____

13. 1000 – 700 = _____

14. 1000 – 730 = _____

15. 1000 – 735 = _____

16. 1000 – 500 = _____

17. 1000 – 550 = _____

18. 1000 – 555 = _____

19. 1000 – 55 = _____

20. 1000 – 5 = _____

21. 1000 – 957 = _____

22. 1000 – 671 = _____

23. 1000 – 860 = _____

24. 1000 – 87 = _____

25. 1000 – 30 = _____

26. 2000 – 30 = _____

27. 2000 – 345 = _____

28. 9000 – 582 = _____

29. 999 + 1 = _____

30. 621 + 379 = _____

Part 4: Two-step Word Problems (pp. 36-38)   2 sessions

Objectives

- Solve simple two-step word problems using pictorial models.

Homework

- Workbook Exercise 13
- Review 1

Notes

In *Primary Mathematics 2* and earlier in *Primary Mathematics 3A*, students solved word problems involving 2 steps where they were given both steps, (a) and (b), and the solution for (b) required the answer from (a). In this section, students will have to determine the intermediate step themselves. Modeling (part-whole or comparison or a combination) can be used to help solve the problems. Use modeling in class work, but do not require students to model solutions in the homework if they can write the equations and determine an answer without actually drawing the model. Students who consistently get problems wrong should be required to draw models.

Activity 2.4a   **Word problems**

1. Discuss the problems on **textbook p. 36,** and **tasks 1-2, textbook p. 37**.
   - As you discuss the problems, model each step. It is important for students to see a step-by-step process, rather than just the finished model. Draw models for the problem on p. 36 and the one in task 1 on p. 37. Ask students pertinent questions such as:
     o What do we need to find out?
     o What information do we need to have in order to solve the problem?
     o How can we get this information?
     o What do we know?

   - On p. 36, in order to find the number of flowers left, we need to know the total number of flowers picked by the two girls. We can draw two part-whole models, or combine them into one model, as shown here.
   - More capable students might see an alternate solution from his diagram. If 20 were given away, then all of Jamie's flowers and 3 of Lindsey's flowers were given away. 12 – 3 = 9.

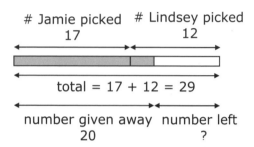

   - For #1 on p. 37, we are finding how many more boys than girls there are, that is, we are comparing girls to boys. We can draw a comparison model to show what they need to find. From it, we can tell that we need to find the number of boys. If necessary, they can draw a part-whole model to find the number of boys.

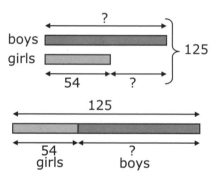

   - Provide some other word problems and have students draw the models for each. You can give some problems that are based on the same information to illustrate the different ways to model them. For example:
     o There are red and blue marbles in a bag. There are 130 red marbles and 40 more blue marbles than red marbles. How many marbles are there in the bag? (300)
     o There are 170 blue marbles in a bag. There are 40 fewer red marbles than blue marbles in the bag. How many marbles are there in the bag? (300)
     o There are 300 marbles in the bag. 130 of them are red and the rest are blue. How many more blue marbles are there than red marbles? (40)
     o There are 300 marbles in a bag. 170 of them are blue and the rest are red. How many fewer red marbles are there than blue marbles? (40)
     o There are 300 red and blue marbles in a bag. There are 40 more blue marbles than red marbles. How many red marbles are there? (130)

Workbook Exercise 13

Activity 2.4b   **Word problems**

1. Have students work independently on some problem from **Practice 2E, textbook p. 38**, and then have them share their solutions. Students should attempt to draw models for all of these. Discuss any alternate approaches students may have. Some possible models are shown for selected problems below.

#1. Number of duck eggs = 1930 – 859 = 1071
     Total eggs = 1930 + 1071 = 3001
     He collected 3001 eggs.

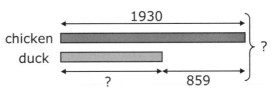

#2. Number of girls = 4100 – 2680= 1420
     Number more boys = 2680 – 1420= 1260
     There were 1260 more boys than girls.
     (Note: The first step is to find the number of girls. We are given a total and one part, the number of boys, so we can draw a part-whole model. Then we need to compare the number of boys to the number of girls, so we can draw a comparison model. Students may draw just one comparison model, and show the total with a bracket.)

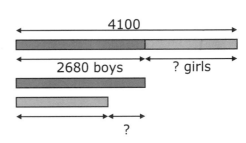

#6. Money in bank = $2467 + $133
                   = $2600
     More money needed
         = $3000 – $2600
         = $400
     She must deposit $400 more.
     (Note: If necessary, two separate drawing can be made, one for each step.

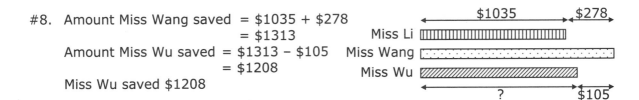

#8. Amount Miss Wang saved = $1035 + $278
                             = $1313
     Amount Miss Wu saved = $1313 – $105
                          = $1208
     Miss Wu saved $1208

Workbook Review 1

Unit 3 – Multiplication and Division

Objectives

- Review multiplication and division facts for 2, 3, 4, 5, and 10.
- Multiply a number by 0.
- Solve 1-step and 2-step word problems involving multiplication and division.
- Use part-whole and comparison models to represent word problems.
- Understand the terms **product**, **quotient**, and **remainder**.
- Multiply and divide numbers within 1000 by 2, 3, 4, or 5 using the formal algorithm.

Suggested number of sessions: 23

	Objectives	Textbook	Workbook	Activities
Part 1 : Looking Back				**4 sessions**
23	▪ Review multiplication concepts. ▪ Review multiplication facts for 2, 3, 4, 5, and 10.	p. 39 p. 40, task 1	Ex. 14-15	3.1a
24	▪ Review division concepts. ▪ Review division facts for 2, 3, 4, 5, and 10.	p. 40, task 2	Ex. 16	3.1b
25	▪ Multiply a number by 0. ▪ Divide 0 by a number.	p. 41, tasks 3-4 p. 43, Practice 3A, #1-3	Ex. 17	3.1c
26	▪ Solve simple word problems involving multiplication and division.	p. 42, tasks 5-6 p. 43, Practice 3A, #4-11	Ex. 18	3.1d
Part 2 : More Word Problems				**5 sessions**
27	▪ Represent simple word problems involving division or multiplication with a part-whole model. ▪ Understand and use the concept of a "unit."	p. 47, Practice 3B, #1-6, 8		3.2a
28	▪ Associate multiplication with "how many times as much", or "how many times more" in word problems. ▪ Represent word problems involving division or multiplication with a comparison model.	p. 44 pp. 45-46, tasks 1-3 p. 47, Practice 3B, #7, 9	Ex. 19	3.2b
29	▪ Solve two-step word problems using all 4 operations.	p. 46, task 4	Ex. 20	3.2c
30	▪ Practice.	p. 47, Practice 3B, #10-12		3.2d
31	▪ Practice.	p. 48, Practice 3C		3.2e

	Objectives	Textbook	Workbook	Activities
Part 3 : Multiplying Ones, Tens and Hundreds				**7 sessions**
32	▪ Multiply tens and hundreds by a 1-digit number. ▪ Write multiplication problems vertically.	p. 49 p. 50, task 1	Ex. 21	3.3a
33	▪ Relate the term **product** to multiplication. ▪ Multiply a 2-digit number by 2, 3, 4, or 5 with renaming only in the tens.	pp. 50-51, tasks 2-3	Ex. 22	3.3b
34	▪ Multiply a 2-digit number by 2, 3, 4, or 5.	pp. 51-52, tasks 4-6	Ex. 23	3.3c
35	▪ Practice.	p. 54, Practice 3D		3.3d
36	▪ Multiply a 3-digit number by 2, 3, 4, or 5.	p. 53, tasks 7-9	Ex. 24	3.3e
37	▪ Practice.	p. 55, Practice 3E	Review 2	3.3f
38	▪ Practice.	p. 56, Practice 3F		
Part 4 : Quotient and Remainder				**3 sessions**
39	▪ Understand the concept of a remainder in division. ▪ Relate the terms quotient and remainder to division.	p. 57		3.4a
40	▪ Understand the vertical representation for division (division algorithm).	p. 58, tasks 1-2		3.4b
41	▪ Divide a 2-digit number by 2. ▪ Identify odd and even numbers.	pp. 59-60, tasks 3-6	Ex. 25	3.4c
Part 5 : Dividing Hundreds, Tens and Ones				**4 sessions**
42	▪ Divide a 3-digit number by 2.	pp. 61-62		3.5a
43	▪ Divide a 2-digit number by 2, 3, 4, or 5.	p. 63, tasks 1-3	Ex. 26	3.5b
44	▪ Divide a 3-digit number by 2, 3, 4, or 5.	p. 64, tasks 4-6	Ex. 27	3.5c
45	▪ Practice.	p. 65, Practice 3G p. 66, Practice 3H		3.5d

Part 1: Looking Back (pp. 39-42)   4 sessions

Objectives

- Review multiplication and division concepts.
- Multiply a number by 0.
- Divide 0 by a number.
- Understand that a number cannot be divided by 0.
- Review simple multiplication and division word problems.

Materials

- Small objects that can be displayed, such as counters
- Multilink cubes for students
- Blank multiplication table (see p. 42 in this guide)
- Fact cards
- Number cards 0-10, four sets per group
- Number cubes labeled with 1, 2, 3, 4, 5 and 10, one for each group
- A set of 50 number cards for each group, containing the multiples of 2, 3, 4, 5, and 10

Homework

- Workbook Exercise 16
- Workbook Exercise 17
- Workbook Exercise 18

Notes

In *Primary Mathematics 2*, students learned multiplication as repeated addition, and division as sharing or grouping. Here, these concepts are reviewed, and the conceptual links between multiplication and division are strengthened.

Both multiplication and division are associated with the part-whole concept. Given the number of equal parts and the number in each part (its value); we can multiply to find the whole (total).

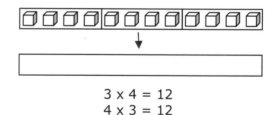

$$3 \times 4 = 12$$
$$4 \times 3 = 12$$

We can always write two related equations for a given multiplication situation.

In *Primary Mathematics*, we study two division situations: sharing and grouping.

Sharing:
A total amount (the whole) is shared into a given number of groups (parts). Divide the total by the number of parts to find the number (value) in each part.

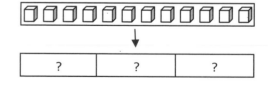

$$12 \div 3 = 4$$

Grouping:
A total amount (the whole) is grouped into equal groups (parts). Divide the total by the number that goes into each part (the value of each part) to find the number of parts.

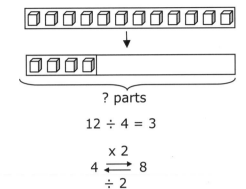

? parts

12 ÷ 4 = 3

Multiplication is related to division. The missing number in __ x 2 = 8 is the answer to 8 ÷ 2 = __.

$$4 \underset{\div\, 2}{\overset{\times\, 2}{\rightleftarrows}} 8$$

In *Primary Mathematics 2*, students learned the multiplication and division facts for 2, 3, 4, 5, and 10.

Multiplication and division of 2, 3, 4, 5 and 10 are reviewed in this section, and multiplication by 0 is introduced. The part-whole concepts of multiplication and division will be used to introduce the use of part-whole and comparison models for multiplication and division in solving word problems.

If the students do not know the multiplication and division facts well, provide plenty of opportunity to practice them. You will be adding in new facts as they are learned in later units. You can have the students create flash cards or use prepared flash cards where the fact (e.g. 3 x 5) is printed on one side, the face, and the answer (e.g. 15) is printed on the other side, the back. They can work in groups, placing the cards face up in the center. Students take turns and point to a card, say the answer, and then turn to card over and check it. If they are correct, they remove the card for that round. Students can practice with the cards individually. You can also use timed or un-timed drill sheets. If there is sufficient class time, you can have the students play games in groups or as a class using large fact cards that can be seen by the whole class. One such game is given here. Suggestions for other games are given later in this guide.

Game:

Prepare cards with answers to the facts being practiced, five per student. Give each student five cards. Students place their cards on their desks face up. Hold up the fact cards one at a time. If a student has a card containing the answer, he or she turns over the card. The student that turns over all five cards first wins.

Multiplication Table

X	1	2	3	4	5	6	7	8	9	10
1										
2										
3										
4										
5										
6										
7										
8										
9										
10										

Activity 3.1a   **Multiplication**

1. Review multiplication concepts.
   - Refer to **textbook p. 39**. See if students can determine what numbers should go on the robots with blank fronts. Lead them to see that in each row the numbers increase by the same amount; i.e. in row 2 the numbers increase by 2.
   - Have students practice counting up by 2's, 3's, 4's, 5's and 10's. You may want to draw a ladder on the board and label the rungs with the multiples. You can then call a multiple of 4 as a member of the 4's-ladder. (The term "multiple" is not formally taught until *Primary Mathematics 4*.)
   - Students should be able to recognize a number as belonging to the sequence of 2's, 3's, 4's, 5's, or 10's. Give students a number that is a multiple of one of these and ask them which "ladder" it belongs to. Help them see how many "ladders" a number can belong to. For example, 12 belongs to the 2, 3, and 4 ladders.
   - Discuss **task 1, textbook p. 40**.
     o Remind students that rather than writing 4 + 4 + 4, we can write 4 x 3 to mean the same thing.
     o Display a 4 by 3 array and show how it can be turned sideways without changing the total. Remind students that 4 x 3 and 3 x 4 give the same answer. So either one can be used for a particular situation.

     4 x 3 ↔ add 4 three times, 4 columns of 3 rows, or 4 + 4 + 4.

     4 x 3 ↔ add 3 four times, 4 rows of 3 columns, or 3 + 3 + 3 + 3.

     3 x 4 ↔ add 3 four times, 3 columns of 4 rows, or 3 + 3 + 3 + 3.

     3 x 4 ↔ add 4 three times, 3 rows of 4 columns, or 4 + 4 + 4.

     So 4 x 3 = 3 x 4

   - Illustrate other similar examples, if necessary. If students need more review, provide them with multilink cubes, write a multiplication sentence, and have them set up the arrays and find the answers.
   - Provide students with a blank multiplication table, such as the one on p. 42 of this guide. Show them how to fill it in with the facts learned so far. Point out that they have already learned most of the multiplication facts. The remaining ones will be learned later. Some students will be able to fill in the rest of the table.

x	1	2	3	4	5	6	7	8	9	10
1	1	2	3	4	5	6	7	8	9	10
2	2	4	6	8	10	12	14	16	18	20
3	3	6	9	12	15	18	21	24	27	30
4	4	8	12	16	20	24	28	32	36	40
5	5	10	15	20	25	30	35	40	45	50
6	6	12	18	24	30					60
7	7	14	21	28	35					70
8	8	16	24	32	40					80
9	9	18	27	36	45					90
10	10	20	30	40	50	60	70	80	90	100

2. Practice math facts.
   - Students should have their own fact cards with which to practice multiplication and division facts. They can use commercial cards or make them in class if there is time, or at home, with index cards and crayons. They can make fact cards for multiplication by 2, 3, 4, 5, and 10. If they are making their own, help the students to first list the facts for the cards they will make.
   - Students may already know these facts well from previous levels and further practice may not be necessary here.
   - Any particular facts they are having trouble with can be included in later fact practice for multiplication by 6, 7, 8, and 9. As students learn the new facts they can add them to their stack of fact cards.

3. **Game**.
   - Divide students into groups. Provide each group with four sets of number cards 1-10 and one number cube labeled with 1, 2, 3, 4, 5, and 10.
   - One person shuffles the cards and deals them all out. Cards should be kept in a pile face down in front of the player. Each player throws a number cube, turns over a card, and multiplies the card's number by the cube's number. Other players check. The player with the largest answer gets all the cards that have been turned over for that round. If there is a tie, the player with the highest number on his card gets the cards. If both players have the same number on their card, then the cards can either stay in the middle for the next round, or they can share them. Play continues until the cards in front of each player are used up. The winner is the one with the most cards.

Workbook Exercises 14 and 15

Activity 3.1b   **Division**

1. Review division concepts.
   - Display 24 objects.
     - ○ Tell students you want to divide 24 objects into 4 groups (or among 4 people). How many will you share into each group? Move the blocks to first put one in each of 4 rows, then another in each row, until they are all shared out.
     - ○ Ask students how many are in each row, or group. (6) Point to the four rows, one by one, and say there are 4 groups of 6.
     - ○ Write 24 ÷ 4 = ___. Remind students that to find the answer to 24 ÷ 4, they can think of the number times 4 that gives 24. Write the corresponding multiplication equation, and show the relationship using arrows. We can "undo" the multiplication by dividing.

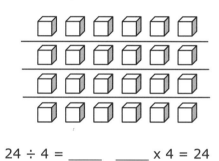

$24 \div 4 =$ _____   _____ $\times 4 = 24$

$6 \times 4 = 24 \rightarrow 24 \div 4 = 6$

   - Keep this array on the board, and repeat the discussion except divide the 24 objects in to 6 groups. Pint out that the new array looks just like the old one turned sideways.

   - Remind students that for each arrangement of objects into groups, we can write two division equations and two multiplication equations. 4 groups of 6 is the same as 6 groups of 4. If we divide 24 into 4 groups, we need 6 in each group. If we need 6 in each group, there will be 4 groups. If we divide 24 into 6 groups, we need 4 in each group. If we need 4 in each group, there will be 6 groups.

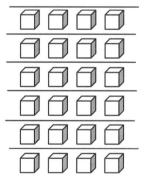

$24 \div 6 = 4$

   - Tell students that in these problems, we are sharing into groups. We know how many groups we want, and are finding how many will go into each group.

$24 \div 4 = 6$
$24 \div 6 = 4$

$4 \times 6 = 24$
$6 \times 4 = 24$

- o For example, we have 24 cookies to share evenly among 4 children. Each child will get 6 cookies. Or we want to share 24 cookies evenly among 6 children. Now each child will get 4 cookies.
- Tell them we still have 24 items, but now we want to group by 4.
  - o For example, we have 24 muffins, and want to put 4 on each plate. How many plates will we need? Illustrate on the board by moving 24 counters into groups, 4 counters in the first group, 4 in the next, and so on. Ask them how many plates we will need. (6).
  - o Whether we are sharing 24 cookies among 4 children to find the number of cookies each child gets, or grouping 24 muffins on to 4 plates to find the number of plates we need, we still get 6 as our answer. In the first case, 6 is the number that each child gets, the number in each group (as in the first array, where a row is one group) or 6 is the number of groups (or plates) we need (as in the second array, where there are 6 rows). So the equation we write for both types of problems is the same, 24 ÷ 4. And for both types of problems, we can find the answer by remembering the multiplication fact 6 x 4 = 24.

> $24 \div 4 = 6$
>
> 24 divided into 4 groups is 6 in each group.
>
> 24 put into groups of 4 each is 6 groups.

2. Discuss **task 2, textbook p. 40**.

3. **Game**:
   - Divide students into groups of 5. Provide each group with a number cube labeled with 1, 2, 3, 4, 5, and 10 and a set of number cards with the multiples of 2, 3, 4, 5, and 10 up to 10 times the number (50 cards) for each group.
   - The dealer shuffles the cards and turns over 5 cards, placing them in the center. Students take turns throwing the cube and getting as many cards from the middle that can be divided evenly by the number on the cube (if a 1 is thrown, the player gets all 5 cards). After each turn, the dealer turns over more cards so that there are always 5 at the beginning of each player's turn. The student with the most cards after all have been turned over wins. They can play the game again with five or six cards in the middle.

Workbook Exercise 16

Activity 3.1c　　　　　　　　　　　　　　　　　　　　　　　**Multiply by 0**

1. Discuss multiplication by 0 and by 1.

   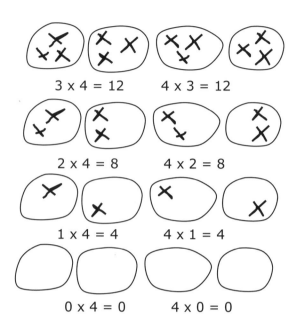

   - Draw 4 circles on the board. Draw 3 X's in each circle.
   - Ask the students for the multiplication sentences and write them on the board.
   - Erase one X from each circle and ask for the new multiplication sentences.

   - Erase another X and repeat.

   - Erase the last X and repeat.

   - Point out that if you have 0 objects in each group, there are 0 objects total.

   - Ask the students for the total if you had 0 groups of 4 objects. Tell them:

      ➢ Zero multiplied by any number is zero.

      ➢ Any number multiplied by zero is zero.

   - Remind students that 1 multiplied by any number is that number. Also, a number divided by 1 is that number.

2. Discuss division of 0 by a number.
   - Use the following situation. There are 0 cookies. You are asked to divide them up among 4 people. How many would each person get? None. If you don't have any cookies, you can't give anyone cookies.
   - Write the equation. Write the related equation as well. Tell them:

      ➢ Zero divided by any number is zero.

      $0 \div 4 = 0 \quad \rightarrow \quad 0 \times 4 = 0$

   - Remind the students that to solve 8 divided by 2, they can think of the number times 2 that is 8. *What* times 2 is 8? **4** x 2 = 8, so 8 ÷ 2 = **4**. But to divide 8 by 0, can they think of a number times 0 that is 8? It does not exist, since any number times 0 is 0. Therefore it is impossible to divide a number by 0. It is not possible to divide 8 into 0 groups, or to count by 0's.

      $8 \div 2 = \underline{\quad} \quad \rightarrow \quad \underline{\quad} \times 2 = 8$

      $8 \div 2 = 4 \quad \rightarrow \quad 4 \times 2 = 8$

      $8 \div 0 = \underline{\quad} \quad \rightarrow \quad \underline{\quad} \times 0 = 8$

3. Have students do **tasks 3-4, textbook p. 41** and **problems 1-3, Practice 3A, textbook p. 43**.
   - Continue providing practice for the multiplication and division facts for 2, 3, 4, 5 and 10, as necessary, through use of mental math worksheets, fact cards, or games. Include multiplication by 0 and division of 0.

Workbook Exercise 17

Mental Math 5

1. 2 x 2 = _____

2. 5 x 5 = _____

3. 4 x 3 = _____

4. 5 x 4 = _____

5. 10 x 5 = _____

6. 2 x 5 = _____

7. 3 x 7 = _____

8. 5 x 9 = _____

9. 2 x 7 = _____

10. 8 x 5 = _____

11. 10 x 2 = _____

12. 5 x 7 = _____

13. 7 x 4 = _____

14. 2 x 9 = _____

15. 9 x 4 = _____

16. 3 x 10 = _____

17. 6 x 5 = _____

18. 6 x 2 = _____

19. 3 x 3 = _____

20. 4 x 4 = _____

21. 0 x 3 = _____

22. 3 x 5 = _____

23. 4 x 2 = _____

24. 8 x 3 = _____

25. 4 x 6 = _____

26. 0 x 10 = _____

27. 9 x 3 = _____

28. 8 x 2 = _____

29. 6 x 3 = _____

30. 4 x 8 = _____

Mental Math 6

1. $50 \div 5 =$ _____

2. $12 \div 3 =$ _____

3. $24 \div 3 =$ _____

4. $20 \div 2 =$ _____

5. $20 \div 5 =$ _____

6. $8 \div 2 =$ _____

7. $24 \div 4 =$ _____

8. $10 \div 10 =$ _____

9. $0 \div 5 =$ _____

10. $18 \div 3 =$ _____

11. $4 \div 4 =$ _____

12. $27 \div 3 =$ _____

13. $14 \div 2 =$ _____

14. $36 \div 4 =$ _____

15. $12 \div 2 =$ _____

16. $16 \div 2 =$ _____

17. $40 \div 4 =$ _____

18. $21 \div 3 =$ _____

19. $6 \div 2 =$ _____

20. $5 \div 5 =$ _____

21. $10 \div 2 =$ _____

22. $25 \div 5 =$ _____

23. $28 \div 4 =$ _____

24. $15 \div 3 =$ _____

25. $10 \div 2 =$ _____

26. $20 \div 4 =$ _____

27. $70 \div 10 =$ _____

28. $0 \div 4 =$ _____

29. $40 \div 5 =$ _____

30. $3 \div 3 =$ _____

Mental Math 7

1. $35 \div 5 =$ _____

2. $7 \times 3 =$ _____

3. $4 \div 2 =$ _____

4. $12 \div 4 =$ _____

5. $10 \times 6 =$ _____

6. $80 \div 10 =$ _____

7. $5 \times 7 =$ _____

8. $45 \div 5 =$ _____

9. $7 \times 10 =$ _____

10. $4 \times 9 =$ _____

11. $3 \times 8 =$ _____

12. $9 \times 2 =$ _____

13. $16 \div 4 =$ _____

14. $0 \div 2 =$ _____

15. $9 \times 3 =$ _____

16. $8 \times 4 =$ _____

17. $9 \div 3 =$ _____

18. $10 \times 9 =$ _____

19. $6 \times 4 =$ _____

20. $5 \div 5 =$ _____

21. $9 \times 5 =$ _____

22. $18 \div 2 =$ _____

23. $0 \times 3 =$ _____

24. $10 \div 5 =$ _____

25. $8 \times 5 =$ _____

26. $30 \div 3 =$ _____

27. $6 \times 5 =$ _____

28. $32 \div 4 =$ _____

29. $4 \times 7 =$ _____

30. $100 \div 10 =$ _____

Activity 3.1d   **Word Problems**

1. Discuss **tasks 5-6, textbook p. 42**. This is a review of word problems than involve multiplication and division.
    *   For task 5, ask the students whether we need to find a total or whether we are given the total. We need to find the total. What information is given? Point out that we are given equal groups (cards) and the number of button (value) in each group. We should multiply to find the total.
    *   For task 6, ask whether we need to find a total or whether are given a total. We are given the total (21 m). What do we need to find? How many parts of 3 meters the total consists of. Point out that we know how many meters need to go into each dress (3 m); we need to find the number of dresses, or how many equal parts.
    *   Task 6 is a division situation involving "grouping." Now, discuss a situation involving "sharing." For example:

        ➢ 4 boys shared $36 equally. How much money did each boy get?

           Point out that we have the total (the total amount of money) and the number of parts (4 boys). We divide to find out how many go into each part.

2. Have students do **problems 4-11, Practice 3A, textbook p. 43**. Students can work on these individually. Call on students to explain their solutions.

3. Provide additional practice. You can include some problems that also involve addition and subtraction situations.

    ➢ There are 35 students in the class. The teacher wants to make 5 teams for a relay race.
        a) How many students will there be in each team?
        b) If 5 students are absent, how many students would there be in each team?

    ➢ There are 6 rows of desks with 4 desks in each row.
        a) How many desks are there?
        b) If there were 30 students in the class, how many more desks would be needed?
        c) How many more desks would be needed if you have to add rows, 4 desks per row, instead of a desk for each student?

    ➢ A book has 50 pages.
        a) If you read 10 pages a day, can you finish the book within a week?
        b) How many days would it take you to read 3 books of the same length if you continued to read 10 pages a day?
        c) If you had borrowed all 3 books from the library and had to return them in two weeks, would you have time to read them all?

    ➢ There are 10 pencils in a pack. The school bought 10 such packs. How many pencils were bought?

    ➢ There are 8 chairs. Each chair has 4 legs. We want to get coasters to put under the legs so they don't scratch the floor. How many coasters do we need?

    ➢ My mother asked me to serve 2 cookies to each of our 5 guests. I looked into the cookie jar and counted 0 cookies, since I had already eaten them. How many could I give each guest?

Workbook Exercise 18

Part 2: More Word Problems (pp. 44-46)   5 sessions

Objectives

- Understand and use the concept of a **unit**.
- Associate multiplication with how many **times as many**, how many **times as much** or how many **times more**.
- Use pictorial models to solve one-step and two-step word problems involving multiplication and division.

Materials

- Objects that can be displayed, such as counters

Homework

- Workbook Exercise 19
- Workbook Exercise 20

Notes

In this topic, students will learn how to use part-whole or comparison models for situations involving multiplication and division.

In a **part-whole model**, the parts are the equal groups. The total is represented with a long bar which can be divided up into equal parts. Each equal part is called a **unit**.

If the problem gives the number of equal parts and the number in each part, divide the total bar into the number of equal parts (units) and label a part with the number in the part (the value). We can see from the model that we must multiply the units to find the total. For example:

There are 4 jars, each with 10 marbles. Find the total number of marbles.

1 unit is the number of marbles in one jar.

    1 unit = 10 marbles

The total number of marbles is 4 units.

    4 units = 10 x 4 = 40 marbles

There are 40 marbles total.

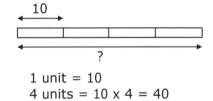

1 unit = 10
4 units = 10 x 4 = 40

If the problem gives a total and the number of equal groups, divide the total bar into the number of equal parts (units) and label the total. We can see from the model that we must divide to find the amount in each unit (its value). For example:

40 marbles are divided equally into 4 jars. Find the number of marbles in each jar.

1 unit is the number of marbles in a jar.

There are 4 units total.

    4 units = 40 marbles

We need to find the number of marbles in 1 unit.

    1 unit = 40 ÷ 4 = 10 marbles

Each jar gets 10 marbles.

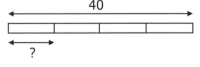

4 units = 40
1 unit = 40 ÷ 4 = 10

If the problem gives the value in each group or part, we can divide to find the number of parts. For example:

There are 40 marbles total. 10 are put into each jar. How many jars are there?

In this problem we don't know the number of units (jars), but we do know the value of each unit (10 marbles). We can find the number of units by division.

40 ÷ 10 = 4

There are 4 jars.

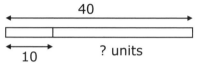

In the **comparison model** for multiplication and division, two quantities are compared. We are told how many times as much one quantity is than the other. The smaller quantity is the unit. We can draw both quantities as a number of equal sized units.

If the problem gives the smaller quantity, which is the amount in one unit, we can see from the model that we find the larger quantity using multiplication. For example:

There are 4 times as many blue marbles in a jar as red marbles. There are 10 red marbles. How many blue marbles are there?

1 unit is the number of red marbles.

1 unit = 10 marbles

Since there are 4 times as many blue marbles as red marbles, there are 4 units of blue marbles.

4 units = 10 x 4 = 40

There are 40 blue marbles.

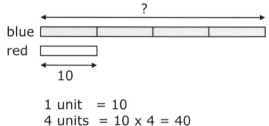

1 unit   = 10
4 units = 10 x 4 = 40

If the problem gives the larger quantity (more than one unit), then we can see from the model that we use division to find the smaller quantity (one unit). For example:

There are 4 times as many blue marbles in a jar as red marbles. There are 40 blue marbles. How many red marbles are there?

1 unit is the number of red marbles.

4 units is the number of blue marbles.

4 units = 40 marbles

We can find the value of 1 unit by division.

1 unit = 40 ÷ 4 = 10 marbles

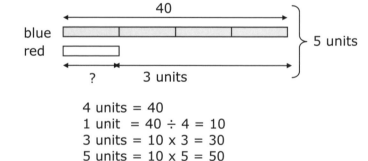

4 units = 40
1 unit = 40 ÷ 4 = 10
3 units = 10 x 3 = 30
5 units = 10 x 5 = 50

Once a unit is found, we can find other amounts, such as how many more one quantity is than another, or the difference between the two quantities, by multiplication of the value of one unit. In the example above, the total number of units is 5, so we can find the total number of marbles by multiplying the value of 1 unit by 5. We could also add the total number of blue marbles to the total number of red marbles. Or, there are 3 more units of blue marbles than red marbles. We can find how many more blue marbles there are than red marbles by multiplying the value of 1 unit by 3. We could also subtract the total number of blue marbles from the total number of red marbles.

In the exercises, the student will encounter two-step word problem involving addition and subtraction as well as multiplication and division. Some of these problems can be modeled using a part-whole model in which one part is a multiple of a unit. From the model, the student can see which operation needs to be used to find the answer to each step of the problem.

If the problem gives one part as a multiple of a given unit, we can find the total by first finding that part through multiplication, then adding the other part. For example:

There 4 small jars, each with 10 marbles, and a can with 15 marbles. How many marbles are there in all?

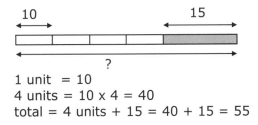

1 unit = 10
4 units = 10 x 4 = 40
total = 4 units + 15 = 40 + 15 = 55

Here we have two parts, the marbles in the small jars and the marbles in the can. We can model the problem by dividing one part into 4 units, labeling the value for 1 unit of one of the parts and labeling the value of the other part. This helps to show that to solve the problem we have to first find the total number of blue marbles. (It is not necessary to label each of the units.)

This type of problem is given in #1 of Exercise 20 in the workbook.

If the problem gives the total and the value of one part and the other part is a multiple of a unit, then we can find the unit by first subtracting to find the unknown part, and then dividing to find the unit. For example:

There are 55 marbles in all. There are 15 marbles in a can. There are 4 jars, each with the same number of marbles. How many marbles are in each jar?

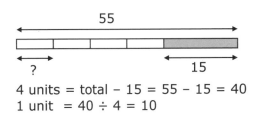

4 units = total – 15 = 55 – 15 = 40
1 unit = 40 ÷ 4 = 10

We can model the problem by drawing it as a bar with two parts. We divide one part into 4 units (for the 4 jars). We can label the bar's total (55), and the value of the other part (15). Now we see that we have to first find the number of marbles in all 4 units, and then divide that by the number of units to find the number of marbles in 1 unit.

This type of problem is given in #2 of Exercise 20 in the workbook.

Learning to do word problems is probably the most valuable skill a student can acquire. Learning to think before calculating — that is, to begin by systematically writing down what is known and what needs to be determined — inculcates this skill as nothing else can. Modeling provides students with systematic means of organizing the information and determining the calculations needed to solve the problem. Make sure your students have adequate practice with modeling. Allow them to see other students' drawing and to compare the models if they differ. The two examples above on this page could, for example, be modeled with two separate bars, as in a comparison model. As the problems become more complex as they move through the *Primary Mathematics* series, students will see that there are several valid ways to solve the same problem, not all of which involve a model such as these. Modeling is, however, a powerful tool that will help them to visualize the problem when they do not know how to approach it or determine what calculations to use.

Activity 3.2a   **Part-whole model for multiplication and division**

1. Represent word problems involving division or multiplication with a part-whole model.
   - Tell the students that they will learn how to diagram multiplication and division problems. Use some problems from the previous lessons to illustrate the use of a part-whole model for solving multiplication and division problems. Write the problems on the board and illustrate the models. Ask questions as you draw the model so that students can see how each part of the model relates to the problem. For example:

   ➢ David bought 4 pineapples at $3 each. How much did he pay altogether?

   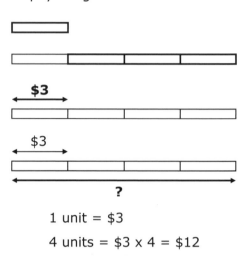

   - How can we show the cost of one pineapple? (with a bar)
   - How many bars should we draw to show the total cost of four pineapples? (4)
   - Each equal part is called a **unit**.
   - What does each pineapple cost? ($3)
   - Label a unit as $3. We don't need to label all the units, since we know they are all the same.
   - What are we trying to find? (the total)
   - Label the whole bar with a question mark.
   - Write an equation to show the amount in 1 unit. (1 unit = $3)
   - How do we find the amount in 4 units? (We multiply the amount in 1 unit by 4.)
   - Write an equation to show the amount in 4 units.
   - David spent $12.

   1 unit = $3

   4 units = $3 x 4 = $12

   ➢ There were 27 desks to clean. 3 boys shared the work equally. How many desks did each boy clean?

   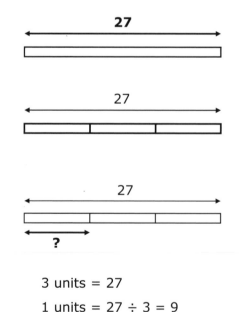

   - We are given a total, the number of desks. We can draw a bar to show this, and label the total amount we have.
   - Since each boy cleaned the same number of desks, and there are 3 boys, we divide the total bar into three parts. We know each part is equal (even if our drawing isn't exact).
   - What does each part stand for? (The number of desks one boy cleans.)
   - We can call each equal part a unit. Units are equal parts.
   - What do we need to find? (The amount of one unit, or the number of desks each boy cleans.) Label that with a question mark.
   - We know the amount for 3 units. What is it? (27) Write an equation to show the amount in 3 units. (3 units = 27)
   - How can we find the number of desks each boy cleans? We divide to get the amount in 1 unit. Write an equation to show the amount in 1 unit.
   - Each boy cleans 9 desks.

   3 units = 27

   1 units = 27 ÷ 3 = 9

➤ Mrs. Nice has 21 mints. She gives each child 3 mints, which uses up all of her mints. How many children did she give mints to?

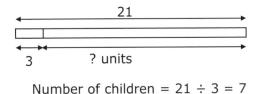

- o What can we make a unit? (The number of mints she gives to each child.)
- o How many units are there? (We don't know.)
- o Do we know the total? (21)
- o We can draw a bar for the total and mark in one unit.
- o How can we find the number of units (children)? (We divide.)

Number of children = 21 ÷ 3 = 7

2. Assign some other problems for students to diagram. Call on students to draw their model on the board.
   - Students can model the problems in **Practice 3A** of the textbook or **Exercise 18** of the workbook.
   - Students can do **problems 1-6 and 8, Practice 3B, textbook p. 47**. They can model #6 and #8.

Activity 3.2b   **Comparison model for multiplication and division**

1. Represent word problems involving division and multiplication with a comparison model.

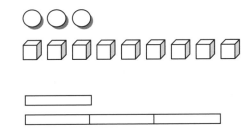

- Display or draw two different kinds of objects, such as counters and blocks. Show three counters. Ask your students for the number of objects that is 3 times as many. Line up blocks under the three counters.
- Draw the pictorial model for the students.
   - o Tell them that each bar we draw is a **unit** and represents 3 objects. Each unit is the same.
   - o Ask students for the number of units drawn for counters and the number of units drawn for blocks. Since there are 3 times as many blocks as counters, the number of units of blocks is 3 times the number of units of counters. Label the bars and the unit.
   - o Ask them how many units show the total number of objects. (4) Write the equations to show that we can find the total number of objects by multiplying the number of units by the amount in each unit. We can also add to find the total.
   - o Ask students, "How many more units of blocks are there than units of counters?" (2) Write the equations showing that we can find the difference between 3 units of blocks and 1 unit of counters. We subtract to find the difference.

Number of counters = 1 unit = 3
Number of blocks = 3 units = 3 x 3 = 9

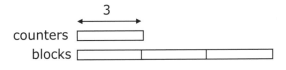

Total = 4 units = 3 x 4 = 12
Total = 3 + 9 = 12

Difference = 2 units = 3 x 2 = 6
Difference = 9 – 3 = 6

2. Discuss the material on **textbook p. 44**.
   - Each square with flowers is a unit. Point out that each unit has the same amount of flowers, both for red flowers and for white flowers.
   - Ask students for two methods to find out how many more red flowers there are than white flowers.
     - There are 27 red flowers and 9 white flowers. 27 – 9 = 18. There are 18 more red flowers than white flowers.
     - There are 2 units more red flowers than white flowers. 1 unit = 9, 2 units = 2 x 9 = 18. There are 18 more red flowers than white flowers.
   - Similarly, ask students for two ways to find the total number of flowers.

3. Discuss **tasks 1-3, textbook pp. 45-46**.
   - Read the whole problems first. Then, draw and label the models as you discuss the problem. Point out that we should draw the units, if we can, before labeling the amounts. For example, in task 1, Meihua has twice as much money as Sulin. This tells us we can draw one bar for Sulin, and then draw Meihua's bar as twice that. Then we can label Meihua's bar from the information in the problem's first sentence (Meihua has $16).

4. Have students do **problems 7-9, Practice 3B, textbook p. 47**. Discuss the solutions.

Workbook Exercise 19

Activity 3.2c   **Two-step word problems**

1. Discuss the following problems with the students, using pictorial models.

   ➢ There are 5 times as many red blocks as blue blocks. There are 4 blue blocks.

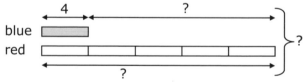

What is 1 unit?	Number of blue blocks = 1 unit
How much is 1 unit?	1 unit = 4 blocks
How many units of red blocks are there?	Number of units of red blocks = 5 units
How many red blocks are there?	5 units = 4 x 5 = 20 blocks There are 20 red blocks.
How many more units of red blocks than blue blocks are there?	There are 4 more units of red blocks than blue blocks.
How many more red blocks than blue blocks are there?	4 units = 4 x 4 = 16 or Difference = 20 – 4 = 16 There are 16 more red blocks than blue blocks.
How many total units are there?	Total blocks = 6 units
How many blocks are there altogether?	6 units = 4 x 6 = 24 or total = 20 + 4 = 24 There are 24 blocks altogether.

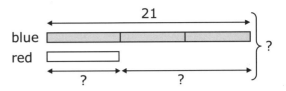

➢ There are 3 times as many blue blocks as red blocks. There are 21 blue blocks.

What is 1 unit?	1 unit = Number of red blocks
How many units of blue blocks are there?	Number of blue blocks = 3 units.
How many blocks are there in 3 units?	3 units = 21 blocks
How many red blocks are there?	1 unit = 21 ÷ 3 = 7 blocks There are 7 red blocks.
How many more units of blue blocks than red blocks are there?	2 units
How many more blue blocks than red blocks are there?	2 units = 7 x 2 = 14 or Difference = 21 - 7 = 14· There are 14 more blue blocks than red blocks.
How many total units are there?	Total blocks = 4 units
How many total blocks are there?	4 units = 7 x 4 = 28 or Total = 21 + 7 = 28 There are 28 blocks in all.

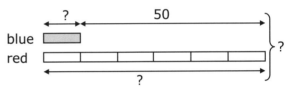

➢ There are five times **more** red blocks than blue blocks. There are 50 more red blocks than blue blocks.

What is 1 unit?	1 unit = Number of blue blocks
How many units **more** red blocks than blue blocks are there?	**More** units of red blocks than units of blue blocks = 5 units
How many units of red blocks are there?	Number of red blocks = 6 units
How many blocks are there in 5 units?	5 units = 50 blocks
How many blocks are there in 1 unit?	1 unit = 50 ÷ 5 = 10 blocks
How many blue blocks are there?	1 unit = 10 blocks There are 10 blue blocks.
How many red blocks are there?	6 units = 10 x 6 = 60 or Number of red blocks = 10 + 50 = 60
How many total units are there?	Total blocks = 7 units
How many total blocks are there?	7 units = 10 x 7 = 70 or Total = 10 + 60 = 70 or Total = 10 + 10 + 50 = 70 There are 70 blocks total.

2. Discuss **task 4, textbook p. 46**. Also discuss an alternative solution:
   - There are 4 more units of chickens than ducks.
        Number of ducks = 1 unit, number of chickens = 5 units
        1 unit = 7; 4 units = 4 x 1 unit = 4 x 7 = 28
        There are 28 more chickens than ducks.
   - You can also ask students for the number of ducks and chickens the farmer has altogether.
        Total ducks and chickens = total chickens + total ducks = 7 + 35 = 42.

Workbook Exercise 20

Activity 3.2d   **Word problems**

1. Discuss the following problems with the students, using pictorial models. Note that although the problems seem complicated, they are easy to solve after the models have been determined.
   - Allow the students to come up with their own models. Students can work on the problems individually and volunteers can demonstrate their solutions to the class. If another student has a different model, allow him or her to show it and compare it to the first student's model. In each case, the student's model should show both what is known and what needs to be determined. One suggested model and solution is given here.
      ➤ Sam bought 4 toy cars and a toy airplane. Each toy car cost $5. The airplane cost $12. How much money did Sam spend altogether? How much more did he spend on the cars than on the airplane?

      There are two parts, the cost of the toy cars and the cost of the toy airplane. The total is the amount of money Sam spent. Draw one part for what he spent on the cars and one for what he spent on the airplane.

      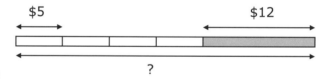

      The airplane cost $12. Label the part for the airplane. The cost of the toy cars is 4 units, one unit for each car. Divide the part for the car into 4 equal units and label one unit. We want to find the total cost, so label that with a question mark.
      To find the total cost, we need to find the total cost of the cars first.
      1 unit = $5 = the cost of 1 toy car.
      Total cost of the cars = 4 units = 4 x $5 = $20
      Total money spent = cost of cars + cost of airplane = $20 + $12 = $32
      Amount more spent on cars = $20 – $12 = $8

      ➤ Mary bought 3 dresses. Each dress cost the same amount. She gave the cashier $20 and got $2 change. How much did each dress cost?

      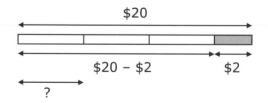

      The total is $20. One part is the change, and the other the cost of the dresses. We want to find the cost of 1 dress. We need to find the cost of all the dresses first.
      Cost of the dresses = $20 - $2 = $18
      Once we find the cost of all the dresses, we can label that.
      Cost of 1 dress = $18 ÷ 3 = $6

➢ Peter has $12. He has twice as much money as Paul. John has $2 less than Paul. How much money does John have?

If John has $2 less than Paul, we need to find out how much money Paul has. We can find that by division.
Paul's money = 1 unit
Peter's money = 2 units = $12
Paul's money = 1 unit
2 units = $12
1 unit = $12 ÷ 2 = $6
John's money = Paul's money - $2 = $6 - $2 = $4

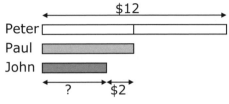

2. Have students do **problems 10-12, Practice 3B, textbook p. 47**.

- #11 can be modeled with 2 parts, one with units. The number graded in the morning is 5 units, or 8 x 5 journals. The total number graded is the sum of two parts, or 40 + 30.

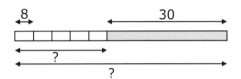

Activity 3.2e   **Practice**

1. Have students do **Practice 3C, textbook p. 48**. Allow them to share their solutions to the word problems.

Part 3: Multiplying Ones, Tens and Hundreds (pp. 49-56)	**7 sessions**

Objectives

- Multiply tens or hundreds by a 1-digit number.
- Write multiplication problems vertically.
- Understand the term **product**.
- Multiply a 2-digit or 3-digit number by 2, 3, 4, or 5.

Materials

- Number discs that can be displayed (1's, 10's, 100's, 1000's)
- Number discs for students
- Place-value charts for students
- Number cards 10, 20, 30, 40, 50, 60, 70, 80, 90, 100, 200, 300, 400, 500, 600, 700, 800, and 900, one set per group
- Number cubes labeled with 2, 3, 4, 4, 5, and 10, one per group
- Number cards 0-9, four sets per group
- Number cubes labeled with 2, 3, 3, 4, 4, and 5, one per group

Homework

- Workbook Exercise 21
- Workbook Exercise 22
- Workbook Exercise 23
- Workbook Exercise 24
- Workbook Review 2

Notes

The multiplication algorithm is introduced here. Only multiplication by 2, 3, 4 or 5 is dealt with in this section; additional multiplication of 2-digit and 3-digit numbers will be dealt with in the next unit as students learn the multiplication facts for 6, 7, 8, and 9.

The algorithm is learned with the use of a place-value chart and number discs. Steps will be given in the activities below. Illustrate as many problems as necessary, one step at a time, with number discs. As you illustrate the steps, write each step down as you proceed so that the students see the connection between the concrete number discs and the numerical representation of each step. Allow students to have access to the base-10 material when doing the problems.

After learning the division algorithm with 2-digit numbers, some students may be able to perform the division mentally by adding the product from the tens to the product from the ones. For example: $34 \times 5 = 150 + 20 = 170$. Allow them to solve problems mentally if they can. If most of your students can do this, provide extra practice with mental multiplication of 2-digit numbers by a 1-digit number.

After this unit is completed, continue to give students several problems involving multiplication of a 3-digit number by a 1-digit number to work on each day for review until the process becomes easy for them. More practice will occur in the unit dealing with multiplication facts for 6, 7, 8, and 9, but if they are already comfortable with the process, they can concentrate on the facts for these numbers.

Mental Math 8

1.   900 x 5 = _____

2.   600 x 2 = _____

3.   70 x 4 = _____

4.   400 x 3 = _____

5.   5 x 700 = _____

6.   70 x 2 = _____

7.   400 x 4 = _____

8.   80 x 3 = _____

9.   90 x 4 = _____

10. 30 x 3 = _____

11. 50 x 5 = _____

12. 800 x 5 = _____

13. 600 x 3 = _____

14. 50 x 4 = _____

15. 1000 x 4 = _____

16. 800 x 4 = _____

17. 50 x 2 = _____

18. 900 x 3 = _____

19. 80 x 5 = _____

20. 90 x 2 = _____

21. 5 x 400 = _____

22. 50 x 3 = _____

23. 400 x 2 = _____

24. 600 x 5 = _____

25. 800 x 2 = _____

26. 3 x 700 = _____

27. 3 x 40 = _____

28. 4 x 600 = _____

29. 20 x 2 = _____

30. 1000 x 5 = _____

Activity 3.3a   **Multiply by tens and hundreds**

1. Illustrate multiplying by tens and hundreds with number discs.
    - Display 2 groups of 3 ones. Ask students how many there would be (total) if there were 2 groups of 3 ones. Write the equation, using ones, and then the standard way.

        3 ones x 2 = 6 ones

        3 ones x 2 = 6 ones
        3 x 2 = 6

    - Then, ask how many there would be if there were 2 groups of 3 tens. Display them and write the equations. Underline the 0's to emphasize that we are multiplying tens.

        3 tens x 2 = 6 tens

        3 tens x 2 = 6 tens
        3<u>0</u> x 2 = 6<u>0</u>

    - Then, ask how many there would be if there were 2 groups of 3 hundreds. Display them and write the equations. Underline the 0's to emphasize that we are multiplying hundreds.

        3 hundreds x 2 = 6 hundreds

        3 hundreds x 2 = 6 hundreds
        3<u>00</u> x 2 = 6<u>00</u>

    - Illustrate a few more similar examples. Include some where there is a 0 from the multiplication, such as 4 x 5. 4 tens x 5 = 20 tens, so there are 3 0's after the 2 in that product.

        4   x 5 = 20
        4<u>0</u> x 5 = 20<u>0</u>
        4<u>00</u> x 5 = 20<u>00</u>

2. Discuss the examples on **textbook p. 49**.
    - Point out that multiplication problems can be written with the numbers on top of each other and the digits aligned. When doing a problem like 400 x 8, the two 0's can be written down first to show that the answer will be hundreds, and then 4 multiplied with 8, and the answer written in the correct places.

        ```
          4 00
        x    8
           00
        ```
        ↓
        ```
          4 00
        x    8
        3 2 00
        ```

    - Illustrate with some additional problems. Only use problems involving the facts for 2, 3, 4, or 5. For example, they can do 800 x 4 or 400 x 8 since the multiplication fact is 4 x 8, but not 600 x 8 since they have not learned the facts for 6 yet. You may also do some problems involving multiplication by 10.

        ```
          5 00
        x   1 0
        5 0 00
        ```

3. Have students do the problems in **task 1, textbook p. 50**.
    - The students should be able to do these mentally. Have them rewrite some of these problems vertically to get used to writing them that way.

4. Provide additional practice as necessary.
   - As you do fact practice activities, you can include problems where the students multiply tens and hundreds by ones.
   - You can use Mental Math 8 and/or games for additional practice.

5. **Game**:
   - Divide students into groups of about four. Provide each group with a number cube labeled with 2, 3, 4, 4, 5, and 10, and the number cards 10, 20, 30, 40, 50, 60, 70, 80, 90, 100, 200, 300, 400, 500, 600, 700, 800, 900. The cards should be shuffled and placed face-down in the middle.
   - Players take turns drawing a card, throwing the number cube, and multiplying the two numbers. They must write the equation. After 3 turns, the players add their three answers. The player with the highest sum wins the round. Reshuffle the cards for each round.

Workbook Exercise 21

Activity 3.3b	**Multiply a 2-digit number**

1. Define the term **product**.
   - Ask students for the answer to 2 x 2. Tell them that the answer to a multiplication problem is called the **product**. Ask them also for the product of 40 x 2. Write the equations 2 x 2 = 4 and 40 x 2 = 80 on the board and have students tell you which of the numbers the product is.

2. Illustrate multiplying a 2-digit number by a 1-digit number with no renaming.
   - Write the multiplication problem 42 x 2. Place the numbers on a place-value chart using number discs.
   - Ask students how they can show this problem with number discs. Double the number of discs on the chart, keeping the two groups of discs distinct.
   - Show students that they can split this problem into two separate problems: 40 x 2 and 2 x 2. We can find the 2 x 2 and the 40 x 2 and add those together to get the final product. Show them how we can write the two parts under the line by thinking of the problem as first 2 x 2, and then 40 x 2.
   - Then show them we can first multiply the ones, write that product down in the ones place, and then multiply the tens and write that product (without the 0) in the tens place, next to the product of the ones.

Hundreds	Tens	Ones
	⑩ ⑩ ⑩ ⑩ ⑩ ⑩ ⑩ ⑩	① ① ① ①
	40 x 2 = 80	2 x 2 = 4

$$\begin{array}{r} 4\,2 \\ \times\quad 2 \\ \hline 4 \leftarrow 2 \times 2 \\ 8\,0 \leftarrow 40 \times 2 \\ \hline 8\,4 \end{array}$$

$$\begin{array}{r} 4\,2 \\ \times\quad 2 \\ \hline 4 \end{array} \rightarrow \begin{array}{r} 4\,2 \\ \times\quad 2 \\ \hline 8\,4 \end{array}$$

2 x 2 = 4   40 x 2 = 80

3. Illustrate multiplying a 2-digit number by a 1-digit number with renaming in the tens only.
   - Put 42 discs on the chart and then triple them by tripling the discs in each place. Show that we can think of 42 as being separated into the tens and ones. We then find the product of each part and add them together.
   - This time multiplying the tens gives 12 tens, which are renamed as 1 hundred and 2 tens.
   - Write each product separately under the line, then show how we can write this in one step, first writing down the product from 2 x 3 in the ones column, then the product of 40 x 3 in the hundreds and tens column.

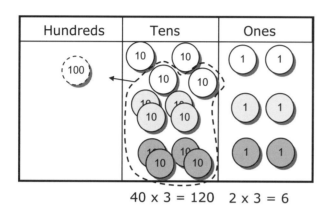

$$40 \times 3 = 120 \quad 2 \times 3 = 6$$

4. Discuss **tasks 2-4, textbook pp. 50-51**.
   - Provide some additional problems for practice. Use problems where there is no renaming or where it only occurs in the tens.

Workbook Exercise 22

Activity 3.3c   **Multiply a 2-digit number**

1. Illustrate multiplying a 2-digit number by 2, 3, 4 or 5 with renaming in the ones.
   - Write the problem 25 x 3, where renaming will occur in the ones. Show the number with number discs on a place value chart.
   - Triple the number of 10-discs and 1-discs on the chart. With the students, work out the problem as shown here.
   - Point out that an extra ten comes from the product of the ones and 3.

Hundreds	Tens	Ones
	10 10	1 1 1
	10	1 1
	10 10	1 1 1
	10 10	1 1

$$20 \times 3 = 60 \quad 5 \times 3 = 15$$

$$
\begin{array}{r}
2\,5 \\
\times \quad 3 \\
\hline
1\,5 \leftarrow 5 \times 3 \\
6\,0 \leftarrow 20 \times 3 \\
\hline
7\,5
\end{array}
$$

- Remove the discs except for the original 25. Tell your students that we will now do the problem in steps.
  (1) Triple just the number of 1-discs: 5 ones x 3 = 15 ones = 1 ten 5 ones. Put 2 more groups of five 1-discs on the chart.
  (2) On the chart, trade in 10 ones for a ten and place the new ten at the top of the chart. Move the 10-disc to the top of the chart. On the written problem, in the ones column, put 5 under the line. Put the 1 we got from re-naming the 10 ones above the tens column. Tell students that this is the usual way to remind ourselves that we have collected a renamed ten.

5 ones x 3 = 15 ones = 1 ten 5 ones

  (3) Now we triple just the number of 10-discs. Put 2 more groups of two 10-discs on the chart. Point out that we only multiply the tens we started with, not the ten that was renamed: 2 tens x 3 = 6 tens.
  (4) Add these 6 tens to our renamed ten: 6 tens + 1 ten = 7 tens.

2 tens x 3 = 6 tens
6 tens + 1 ten = 7 tens

- Illustrate other examples where there is renaming only in the ones.
- Discuss **task 4, textbook p. 51**.

2. Illustrate multiplying a 2-digit number by 2, 3, 4 or 5 with renaming in the ones and tens.
   - Discuss **task 5, textbook p. 52**. In this example, the tens are also renamed, since we have 10 tens.

- Illustrate another problem where both ones and tens are renamed. Show each step of the problem both with the discs and on the written problem.

$$
\begin{array}{r}
\mathbf{2} \\
6\,5 \\
\times\ \ 4 \\
\hline
0
\end{array}
\qquad\longrightarrow\qquad
\begin{array}{r}
2 \\
6\,5 \\
\times\ \ 4 \\
\hline
2\,6\,0
\end{array}
$$

$(5 \times 4 = 20)$ $(60 \times 4 = 240$
                                          $240 + 20 = 260)$

3. Have students do **task 6, textbook p. 52**.

Workbook Exercise 23

Activity 3.3d   **Practice**

1. Use **text p. 54, Practice 3D** to review and practice concepts learned so far.

2. **Game**:
    - Divide students into groups. Give each group 4 sets of number cards 0-9, shuffled, and a number cube labeled with 2, 3, 3, 4, 4, and 5. The dealer deals out all the cards.
    - Players turn over two cards to form a 2-digit number. The first card turned over is the tens, and the second card is the ones. They then throw the cube and multiply the 2-digit number by the number on the cube. They must record their multiplication equation. The player with the highest product gets a point.

Activity 3.3e   **Multiply a 3-digit number**

1. Illustrate multiplying a 3-digit number by 2, 3, 4 or 5.
    - Write the expression 476 x 3.
    - Draw a line on a place-value chart near the top and place the discs for 476 under this line.

Thousands	Hundreds	Tens	Ones

476
x   3

(1) First multiply the ones by 3. Ask students for the product of 6 ones and 3. Rename the answer as tens and ones. 6 ones x 3 = 18 ones = 1 ten 8 ones. Put three times as many ones on the chart.

(2) On the chart, trade in 10 ones for 1 ten and place it above the line you drew to keep it separate from the other tens.
On the written problem, put an 8 in the ones place under a line and a 1 above the tens place. Remind students that this is to remind us that we have a renamed ten from multiplication of the ones.
If it will help the students' understanding you may also want to write the entire product under the line to show how it compares to writing the renamed tens above.

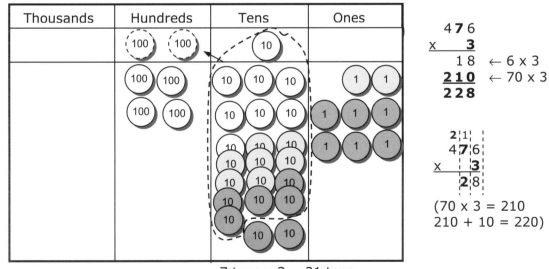

Thousands	Hundreds	Tens	Ones

476
x   3
18 ← 6 x 3

1
47**6**
x   **3**
  8

(6 x 3 = 18)

6 ones x 3 = 18 ones = 1 ten 8 ones

(3) Now, multiply the tens by 3. Ask students for the product of 7 tens and 3. Remind them that we only multiply the original tens (7), and do not include any tens that came from multiplying the ones. Write the product as 7 tens x 3 = 21 tens
On the chart, put three times as many tens.

(4) Add the tens that came from renaming the ones. Tell students that this can be done mentally — think of the product of 7 and 3 (21) and count up one more to get 22. This gives the total number of tens. Rename these tens as hundreds and tens. 22 tens = 2 hundreds 2 tens.

(5) On the chart, trade in 20 tens for 2 hundreds. Place them on the chart separately from the hundreds already there.
On the written problem, write the 2 tens in the tens column under the line and the 2 renamed hundreds above the hundreds place.

Thousands	Hundreds	Tens	Ones

476
x   3
  18 ← 6 x 3
210 ← 70 x 3
228

2 1
47**6**
x   **3**
2 8

(70 x 3 = 210
210 + 10 = 220)

7 tens x 3 = 21 tens
21 tens + 1 ten = 22 tens = 2 hundreds 2 tens

(6) Tell students that so far we have 228 from multiplying the ones and tens. Ask students for the next step. We now multiply the hundreds by 3. We only multiply the original hundreds (4); not the two that were renamed. Ask them for the product of four hundreds and 3: 4 hundreds x 3 = 12 hundreds.

(7) Put three times as many hundreds on the chart. Ask them for the total number of hundreds now. They need to add in the 2 hundreds that came from renaming. Tell them they can do these steps by thinking 4 x 3 = 12, and then counting up 2 more to add in the extra 2 hundreds; 13, 14 — so we have 14 hundreds.

(8) Trade in 10 hundreds for 1 thousand and place it on the chart.
Since there are no thousands to be multiplied, write the thousands and the hundreds below the line on the written problem.

$$
\begin{array}{r}
4\,7\,6 \\
\times \quad 3 \\
\hline
1\,8 \quad \leftarrow 6 \times 3 \\
2\,1\,0 \quad \leftarrow 70 \times 3 \\
\hline
2\,2\,8 \\
1\,2\,0\,0 \quad \leftarrow 400 \times 3 \\
\hline
1\,4\,2\,8
\end{array}
$$

$$
\begin{array}{r}
{}^{2\,1} \\
4\,7\,6 \\
\times \quad 3 \\
\hline
1\,4\,2\,8
\end{array}
$$

(400 x 3 = 1200
1200 + 200 = 1400)

4 hundreds x 3 = 12 hundreds
12 hundreds + 2 hundreds = 14 hundreds = 1 thousand 4 hundreds

Now, we have 1428 from multiplying the ones, tens, and hundreds.

$$
\begin{array}{r}
{}^{2\,1} \\
4\,7\,6 \\
\times \quad 3 \\
\hline
1\,4\,2\,8
\end{array}
$$

- Illustrate the example in **task 7, textbook p. 53**.
- Step through the multiplication algorithm with **task 8, textbook p. 43**, without discs. If students need more concrete help, use discs.

2. Have students solve the problems in **task 9, textbook p. 53**. Allow students that need it to use a place-value chart and discs, or to draw circles on a place-value chart, until they can do it without the chart. Give additional problems as necessary.

Workbook Exercise 21

Activity 3.3f   **Practice**

1. Use **Practice 3E, textbook p. 55,** and **Practice 3F, textbook p. 56,** to review
    multiplication of a 2-digit or a 3-digit number by a 1-digit number.
    *   Call on students to explain their solutions to the word problems.

2. **Game**:
    *   Divide students into groups. Give each group 4 sets of number cards 0-9, shuffled, and
        a cube labeled with 2, 3, 3, 4, 4, and 5. The dealer deals all the cards.
    *   Players turn over three cards to form a 3-digit number. The first card turned over is the
        hundreds, the next is the tens, and the third is the ones. They then throw the cube.
        They multiply the 2-digit number by the number on the cube. They must record their
        multiplication equation. The one with the highest product gets a point.

Workbook Review 2

Part 4: Quotient and Remainder (pp. 57-60)	3 sessions

Objectives

- Understand the remainder in division.
- Divide a 2-digit number by 2.
- Relate the terms **quotient** and **remainder** to division.
- Identify odd and even numbers.

Materials

- Number discs that can be displayed (1's, 10's, 100's)
- Number discs for students
- Paper bowls or plates, 5 per student (or loops of yarn or paper divided into 5 regions)
- Hundreds board that can be displayed
- Hundreds boards for students (copied or laminated boards and dry-erase markers)
- Number cards 0-9, four sets per group

Homework

- Workbook Exercise 25

Notes

Starting with page 39 in the textbook, we have linked the concept of division with the familiar processes of addition and multiplication. Now, we are ready to introduce a new concept that applies only to division: that the application of division includes the possibility of division into unequal parts, with the resulting remainder.

The concept of remainder and its application to the division algorithm is introduced through division by 2. The division algorithm is a step-by-step process in which the digit in the highest place value is divided first, and the remainder renamed and included in the division of the digit in the next place value.

The division algorithm is a relatively complex process for students since it requires understanding all four operations, with constant attention to place value. Spend adequate time on this concept, and allow students access to place value charts, number discs, and base-10 material until they thoroughly understand the process. Encourage them to get into the habit of checking their answers with number discs or base ten materials, or by pencil and paper computation.

After practice, some students may be able to divide a 2-digit number by 2 mentally. Allow them to use mental techniques if they are able to, but do not make this a requirement.

Activity 3.4c could take 2 days to do.

Activity 3.4a

Quotient and remainder

1. Introduce quotient and remainder using number discs.

   • Display 8 1-discs. Tell the students that Julie has 8 marbles and wants to share them with a friend equally. Write the equation as 8 ÷ 2 = 4.

   • Tell students that when we divide into equal parts, the answer is called the **quotient**. Say and write the word <u>quotient</u> and have students copy it.

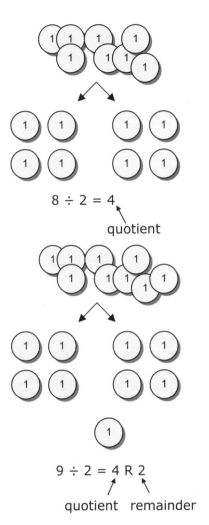

   • Display 9 1-discs now. Tell the students that Charlie has 9 marbles which he would like to share equally with a friend. Write "9 ÷ 2". Move the discs into 2 piles as while you say "Charlie counts out: 1 for me, 1 for you, 1 for me, 1 for you… But he has to stop because there is one left over." Tell students that in division we have a special name for "left over." We call it the **remainder**. Say and write the word <u>remainder</u> and have students copy it.

   • Tell them that the answer to a division problem with a "left over" is written a special way. Write the equation on the board: 9 ÷ 2 = 4 R 1. The 4 is the quotient (for equal parts), R tells us that the number after it is the remainder, and the 1 after the R is the remainder (the left-over part).

   • Discuss **textbook, p. 57**. Note that if each tent gets 3 toy soldiers, there will be 2 left over.
     ○ 12 of the toy soldiers were divided into equal groups, but if the two left over are put into any of the groups, the groups would not be equal any more. Tell them that we write this as 14 ÷ 4 = 3 R 2. 3 is the quotient and 2 is the remainder.

   • Tell them they now know the special name that the answer has for all four operations: addition, subtraction, multiplication, and division. Ask them for the name of the answer in addition (sum), subtraction (difference), multiplication (product), and division (quotient and remainder).

   • Remove the discs. Write the equation 8 ÷ 2 = ?. Remind students that in order to find the answer they can think of the number times 2 that gives 8. It is 4.

   • Write the equation 9 ÷ 2 = ?. Tell them that they know that there isn't a number times 2 that gives 9. To answer the problem, they have to think of the number times 2 that gives the number closest to 9. 4 x 2 = 8. Then to find the remainder, they find the difference between 8 and 9. The remainder is 1.

8 ÷ 2 = ?	4 x 2 = 8
8 ÷ 2 = 4	
9 ÷ 2 = ?	4 x 2 = 8
9 ÷ 2 = 4 R 1	8 + 1 = 9

- Students need to have a thorough understanding of remainders to adequately perform the division algorithm successfully. They need to be able to easily find remainders using multiplication and division facts they already know. Provide plenty of practice in finding remainders based on division facts they are already familiar with, i.e. the facts up to 10 x 5. Give them other division problems with 1-digit quotients where there is a remainder. Only use problems where the divisor is 2, 3, 4, or 5. Guide students in finding the quotient and then the remainder. You may want to let them use number discs and cups or paper plates to act out the problems initially. Eventually they should be able to find remainders for simple problems without the discs.

  - For example, in finding 23 ÷ 5, they need to find the number closest to 23 that they would get when multiplying another number by 5. They can count up by 5's to find it, 5, 10, 15, 20, 25. 25 is more than 23, so the closest number has to be 20. What times 5 is 20? Or, 20 divided by 5 is what number? It is 4. The quotient is 4. What is the remainder? It is 3.

$$23 \div 5 = ?$$
$$20 \div 5 = ?$$
$$? \times 5 = 20 \qquad ? = 4$$
$$23 \div 5 = 4 \text{ r } 3$$
$$20 + 3 = 23$$
$$4 \times 5 = 20 \quad 3$$
$$23$$

$$23 \div 4 = \text{quotient} + \text{remainder}$$
$$4 \times \text{quotient} + \text{remainder} = 23$$

Activity 3.4b   **Division the vertical way**

1. Introduce the vertical representation for division.
   - Review the terms quotient and remainder. In division when we divide into equal parts, the answer is called the *quotient*. Say and write the word <u>quotient</u> and have the students copy it. We have a special name for "left over." We call it the *remainder*. Say and write the word <u>remainder</u> and have the students copy it.
   - Tell students that they are going to learn to write division problems a new way. Write the equation 24 ÷ 4 = 6 (elicit the answer from the students). Draw the symbol $\overline{)}$.

     Explain that we put the number we are dividing (24) inside the open box (do so on the board). We put the number we are dividing by (4) to the left of the curved side (do so). We put the quotient to the division problem on the top of the box (do so). Point out that all the digits except the number of groups or parts are lined up according to place value. The quotient is 6 ones, so it goes in the ones place or column. You can separate the digits in each place-value column with a dotted line. Also point out that the quotient (6) times the number outside the box (the 4) equals the number inside the box (24).
   - Give students some other division problems (without remainders) and have them find the quotient and rewrite the problem the new way.

$$24 \div 4 = 6$$

$$\overline{)2\ 4}$$

$$4\overline{)2\ 4}$$

$$4\overline{)2\,|\,4}^{\ \ \,|6}$$

$$21 \div 3 = 7 \qquad 3\overline{)2\,|\,1}^{\ \ |7}$$

$$36 \div 4 = 9 \qquad 4\overline{)3\ 6}^{\quad 9}$$

- Write a problem which will involve a remainder using the symbol $\overline{)}$. From previous practice students should be able to easily find the quotient and remainder. Step through the process, showing where each step should be recorded.

  - o Step 1: Find the quotient. If 23 were divided into 3 parts how many can go into each part equally? Or, what number times 3 gives the number closest but less than 23? Write this number above the line.
  - o Step 2: Write the number that could be evenly divided below the number in the box. This number is 7 x 3. Line the digits up – tens below tens and ones below ones.
  - o Step 3. Subtract this product from the total. Draw a line under the two numbers and write the difference down. This is the remainder. You can write R followed by the remainder above the line.

2. Discuss the top of **textbook p. 58** and **tasks 1-2, textbook p. 58**.
   - Have students identify each number in the vertical representation.
   - Students sometimes find this vertical representation difficult and forget where each step should be written. They should thoroughly understand this process or they will get confused later. Provide some other division problems with 1-digit quotients where there is a remainder and have the students write the problem vertically, including the number that can be divided evenly under the total and the remainder below that.

Activity 3.4c   **Division algorithm**

1. Divide a 2-digit number by 2, using the division algorithm.
   - Provide students with number discs and two paper bowls or plates or other means of keeping groups separate. Use number discs or base-10 blocks to illustrate the steps as the students do them. Go through the division algorithm step-by-step with them, showing how the steps are represented. A suggested procedure is given here.
   - Students should copy the equation.

   Ask students to pick out 5 tens and 3 ones. Then, write the equation using the symbol $\overline{)}$.

   Step 1: Tell the students that we first divide the tens and get the quotient and remainder for the tens. How many tens go into each of the 2 groups? (2) Move the discs into the two groups. This is the <u>quotient for the tens</u> and we write it above the line the tens place. How many were divided successfully into two groups (4 tens). We write that number under the total in the tens column so that we can subtract it from the tens we had. The <u>remainder tens</u> is 1 ten; that is, the 2 and the 4 are tens and the <u>remainder</u> 1

is also a ten. The 2 and the 4 and remainder 1 are tens. We write all of them in the tens column.

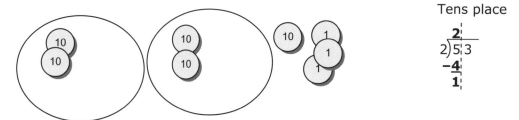

Step 2: The next step is to combine the <u>remainder tens</u> with the ones so that we can divide them. We rename the ten as ten ones.
Replace the 10-disc with ten 1-discs. We add the ten ones to the 3 ones we started with. What is the total we still need to divide up? (13) We show this on the written problem by writing the 3 after the remainder from dividing the tens. The total remainder is 13.

Also show this to the students by making a number bond with 53, the tens that were divided up so far, and the remainder.

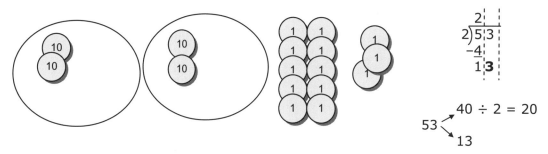

Step 3: Tell students that the next step is to divide the 13 ones into 2 groups. Move the 1-discs into the two groups. How many go in each group? (6)
We write the number of ones that goes into each group above the box in the ones column. How many did we successfully divide up? We can find this by multiplying 6 and 2. (12) We write this 12 under the 13 so that we can subtract it from 13 to show the <u>remainder</u>.
Add this new division to the number bond representation.

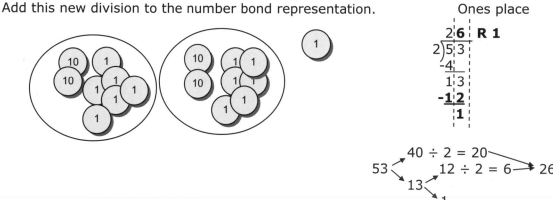

- Review the steps for the students. We first divide the tens and find the remainder. We rename the remainder as ones and then divide the ones. The quotient is the quotient from dividing both tens and the ones.
- Write and illustrate another problem.

2. Discuss **tasks 4-5, textbook pp. 59-60**.
   - Give students additional problems. Allow them to use number discs for some problems if they need it, but also provide practice without number discs.

3. Identify odd and even numbers.
   - Provide students with number discs (1's). Have them count out 2 discs, and then divide them into two separate piles. You can do the same using discs on the board or overhead. Write the division equation and have students give you the answer. 2 ÷ 2 = 1. Repeat with 4, 6, 8, and 10.
   - Tell students that if a number can be divided by 2 without a remainder, it is an **even** number.
   - Now have the students count out one 1- disc and ask them to divide it into two separate piles. Obviously, they can't. Write the division equation: 1 ÷ 2 = 0 R 1. Ask them to divide 3, 5, 7, and 9 into two groups and write the equations. For example: 5 ÷ 2 = 2 R 1.
   - Tell students that if a number divided by 2 results in a remainder, it is an **odd** number.
   - Display a hundreds board. Provide students with copied hundreds boards they can mark. Have them count by 2's on the hundreds board, and circle all the numbers they land on.
     - Pick a few of the circled numbers and have students divide them by 2. Ask them whether they are odd or even. Since there is no remainder, they are even.
     - Pick a few of the numbers not circled and divide them by 2. Ask students whether they are odd or even. Since there is a remainder, they are odd.
     - Ask students if they can see a pattern. All the marked numbers end in 0, 2, 4, 6, or 8. The unmarked numbers end in 1, 3, 5, 7, or 9.
   - Discuss **task 6, textbook p. 60**.
   - Remind students that an even number when divided by 2 leaves no remainder. Ask them whether they think 0 is even or odd. By this definition, 0 is even. 0 divided by 2 is 0 and there is no remainder.

4. **Game**:
   - Divide students into groups of four. Provide each group with 4 sets of number cards 0-9, shuffled. Cards are placed face down in the middle.
   - For each round, student take turns turning over 2 cards to form a 2-digit number. The first card is the tens, and the second the ones. The students divide their numbers by 2 and record their answer. After 3-5 rounds, they find the sum of their quotients and also add in any remainders. The student with the highest sum wins.

Workbook Exercise 25

Hundreds Board

1	2	3	4	5	6	7	8	9	10
11	12	13	14	15	16	17	18	19	20
21	22	23	24	25	26	27	28	29	30
31	32	33	34	35	36	37	38	39	40
41	42	43	44	45	46	47	48	49	50
51	52	53	54	55	56	57	58	59	60
61	62	63	64	65	66	67	68	69	70
71	72	73	74	75	76	77	78	79	80
81	81	83	84	85	86	87	88	89	90
91	92	93	94	95	96	97	98	99	100

Part 5: Dividing Hundreds, Tens and Ones (pp. 61-67)   **4 sessions**

Objectives

* Divide a 2-digit or 3-digit number by 2, 3, 4, or 5.

Materials

* Number discs that can be displayed (1's, 10's, 100's)
* Base-10 blocks that can be displayed
* Base-10 blocks for students
* Number discs for students
* Paper plates, 5 per student (or 5 paper bowls, napkins, loops of yarn or paper divided into 5 regions)
* Hundreds board that can be displayed
* Hundreds boards for students (3 paper copies per student or a laminated board and dry-erase markers)
* Number cards 0-9, four sets per group
* Number cube labeled with 3, 3, 4, 4, 5, and 5, one per group
* Number cube with 2, 3, 3, 4, 4, and 5, one per group
* Opaque bag to hold number discs, one per group

Homework

* Workbook Exercise 26
* Workbook Exercise 27

Notes

In this section, students will first divide a 3-digit number by 2 by extending the concepts learned in the last section for dividing a 2-digit number by 2. Then they will use the same process to divide a 2-digit or 3-digit number by 3, 4, or 5. Allow them to use base-10 material until they are comfortable with the process. More capable students may develop a short-hand method of writing the division algorithm where they only put the remainder under the total amount. Use discretion in requiring students to record all steps. Mental math increases a student's flexibility in understanding and working with numbers. This is true even if some steps are done mentally but not all. However, students should not leave out steps just because they don't want to write as much if that results in a higher error rate.

Activity 3.5a   **Division algorithm**

1. Divide a 3-digit number by 2.
   • Provide students with base-10 blocks or number discs and two paper plates or bowls. Follow a procedure similar to that in the **textbook, pp. 61-62**. Write the solutions of the problems vertically, and illustrate the steps with number discs.
   • Have students pick out 4 hundreds, divide them into two groups, and copy the problem you have written on the board. Point to each part of the written problem and ask them to identify what that part represents.

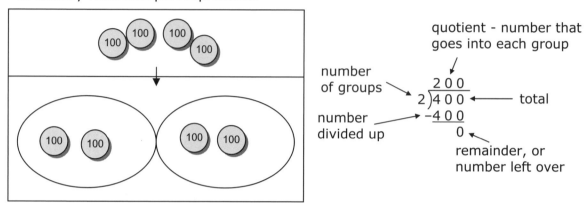

   • Now ask students to pick out 5 hundreds and put them into two groups. Show them how to write down the steps.
      ○ First they must divide as many hundreds into 2 groups as they can (2 hundreds in each), and find the remainder (1 hundred).
      ○ Rename the remainder as 10 tens, and then divide the tens into 2 groups (5 tens in each) and find the new remainder (0).
      ○ Note when each digit is written in a particular column; for example, the 2 of the quotient from dividing the hundreds is written in the hundreds place above the box.

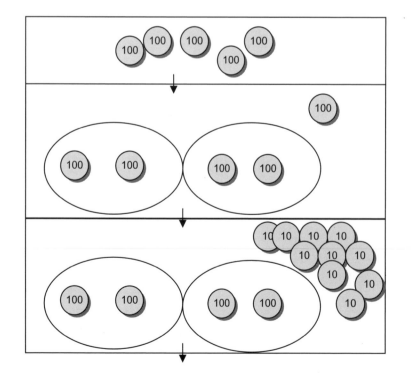

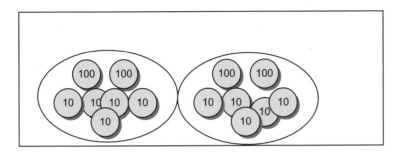

Tens place

$$2\,5\,0$$
$$2\overline{)5\,0\,0}$$
$$\underline{-4}$$
$$1\,0$$
$$\underline{-1\,0} \quad \leftarrow 2 \times 50$$
$$0$$

- Now, ask students to pick out 5 hundreds and 5 tens and put them into two groups, first dividing up the hundreds, and then the tens, and then the ones.
  - Show them how to write down the steps. This time, there are tens to add to the remainder from dividing the hundreds, so there are 15 tens instead of 10 tens. We show this by "bringing down the 5" by writing the 5 tens next to the first remainder. Every time a remainder is found, the next digit in the next lower place value is written next to it.
  - When we divide up the tens, the quotient is now 7 tens and there is a remainder of one ten.
  - We write the next digit in the next lower place value next to the remainder – in this case it is 0. So we have ten ones that are divided up, and now all have been divided so the final remainder is 0.

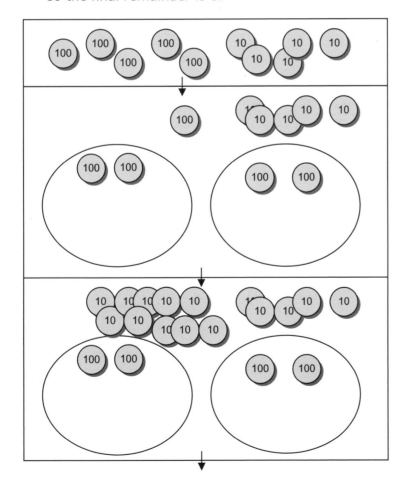

Hundreds place

$$2$$
$$2\overline{)5\,5\,0}$$
$$\underline{4} \qquad \leftarrow 200 \times 2$$
$$1 \qquad \leftarrow \text{remainder hundred}$$

$$2$$
$$2\overline{)5\,5\,0}$$
$$\underline{4}$$
$$1\,5 \qquad \leftarrow \text{total tens}$$

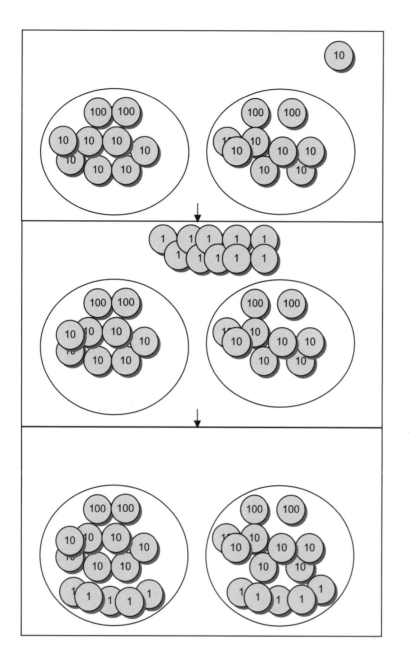

Tens place

```
  2 7
2)5 5 0
  4
  1 5
 -1 4      ← 70 x 2
    1      ← remainder ten
```

```
  2 7 5
2)5 5 0
 -4
  1 5
 -1 4
    1 0    ← total ones
```

Ones place

```
  2 7 5
2)5 5 0
 -4
  1 5
 -1 4
    1 0
   -1 0    ← 5 x 2
      0
```

- Now, ask students to pick out 5 hundreds, 5 tens, and 5 ones and divide them into 2 groups. Follow the same procedure as before. In this case, after dividing the tens and renaming, the total ones is 15. When the ones are divided into two groups, there is a remainder of one.
- Give students other 3-digit numbers to divide by 2. Include some where there are no tens, for example 402 ÷ 2. Illustrate as many as necessary. Have students work on some individually, both with and without base-10 material.

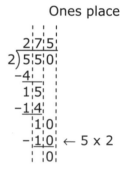

```
   2 7 7  R 1
2)5 5 5
 -4
  1 5
 -1 4
    1 5
   -1 4
       1
```

2. **Game**:
   - Divide students into groups of four. Provide each group with 4 sets of number cards 0-9, shuffled. Cards are placed face down in the middle.
   - For each round, student take turns turning over 3 cards to form a 3-digit number. The first card is the hundreds, the second the tens, and the third the ones. Then students divide their numbers by 2 and record their answer. After three rounds, they find the sum of their quotients and also add in any remainders. The student with the highest sum wins.

Activity 3.5b   **More division**

1. Divide a 2-digit number by 3, 4, or 5.
   - Provide students with number discs.
   - Step through problems involving division of a 2-digit number by 3, 4, or 5. Illustrate each step with number discs.
     - First, tens are divided.
     - Any remaining tens are traded in for ones.
     - All the remaining ones are then divided.
     - Write the problem and point out how each step is recorded — where the quotient goes, where the number successfully divided goes for each step, how to record the remainder and add the digit from the next lower place to the remainder ("bring down the ___").

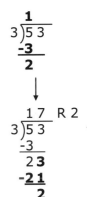

2. Discuss **tasks 1-2, textbook p. 63**.

3. Have students solve the problems in **task 3, textbook p. 63**.

4. **Games**:
   - Divide students into groups of four. Provide each group with 4 sets of number cards 0-10 and a number cube labeled with 3, 3, 4, 4, 5, and 5. Cards are shuffled and all are dealt.
   - Each player turns over two cards to form a 2-digit number. The first card turned over is the tens, the second the ones. Then each player also throws the cube, and divides their number formed by the cards by the number on the cube.
     - Game 1: The student with the highest quotient after each round gets a point. The student with the most points wins.
     - Game 2: After 3-5 rounds, the quotients and remainders are added. The student with the highest sum wins.
     - Game 3: The student with the highest quotient gets all the cards that have been turned over. If there is a tie, the one with the highest remainder gets the cards. Play continues until one student has all the cards, or until all cards are turned over, in which case the student with the most cards wins.

Workbook Exercise 26

Activity 3.5c   **More division**

1. Divide a 3-digit number by 3, 4, or 5.

   - Provide students with base-10 blocks or number discs.
   - Step through problems involving division of a 3-digit number by 3, 4, or 5. Illustrate each step with base-10 material. First hundreds are divided. Any remaining hundreds are traded in for tens. Then all the tens are divided. Any remaining tens are traded in for ones. Then all the ones are divided. Write the problem and point out how each step is recorded.

$$
\begin{array}{r}
\mathbf{1} \\
5\overline{)9\,8\,2} \\
\underline{5} \\
4
\end{array}
$$

$$
\begin{array}{r}
1\,\mathbf{9} \\
5\overline{)9\,8\,2} \\
\underline{5} \\
4\,8 \\
\underline{4\,5} \\
3
\end{array}
$$

2. Discuss **tasks 4-5, textbook p. 64**.

$$
\begin{array}{r}
1\,9\,\mathbf{6}\ \text{R 2} \\
5\overline{)9\,8\,2} \\
\underline{5} \\
4\,8 \\
\underline{4\,5} \\
3\,\mathbf{2} \\
\underline{3\,\mathbf{0}} \\
\mathbf{2}
\end{array}
$$

3. Have students solve the problems in **task 6, textbook p. 64**.

4. **Games**:
   - Divide students into groups of four. Provide each group with 4 sets of number cards 0-10 and a number cube labeled with 3, 3, 4, 4, 5, and 5. Cards are shuffled and all are dealt. If there are four players in a group, this will give enough cards for only 3 rounds, which may be all that is needed. If more rounds are wanted, the cards can be reshuffled.
   - Each player turns over three cards to form a 3-digit number. The first card turned over is the hundreds, the second the tens, and the third the ones. Then each player also throws the cube, and divides their number formed by the cards by the number on the cube.
     - Game 1: The student with the highest quotient after each round gets a point. The student with the most points wins.
     - Game 2: After 3-5 rounds, the quotients and remainders are added. The student with the highest sum wins.
     - Game 3: The student with the highest quotient gets all the cards that have been turned over. If there is a tie, the one with the highest remainder gets the cards. Play continues until one student has all the cards, or until all cards are turned over, in which case the student with the most cards wins.

Workbook Exercise 27

Activity 3.5d   **Word problems, practice**

1. Use **Practice 3G, text p. 65,** and **Practice 3H, text p. 66**. Students can solve problems individually, and then some can present their solutions to the class.

2. Optional: Investigate remainders and divisibility.
   - Provide students with three copied hundreds boards.
   - Review odd and even numbers. You can ask students questions such as the following.
     o Find the number 42. Is it odd or even? (even) How about 61? (odd)
     o Give me an odd number. An even number.
     o What is the remainder if an even number is divided by 2? (0)
     o What is the remainder if an odd number is divided by 2? (1)
     o How can we tell if a number is even or odd without dividing it first? (Even numbers end in 0, 2, 4, 6, or 8)
     o Even numbers are divisible by 2. That means that when you divide the number by 2, there is no remainder. Is 17 divisible by 2? Is 32 divisible by 2?
   - Have students circle the numbers on a hundreds board that they land on when counting up by 3's. Pick out a few of these and have students divide them by 3. Discuss divisibility by three:
     o What is the remainder if one of the circled numbers is divided by 3? (0)
     o Pick a number that is one more than a circled number and divide it by 3. What is the remainder? (1)
     o Pick a number that is one less than a circled number and divide it by 3. What is the remainder? (2)
     o Can we get a remainder of 3 when we divide a number by 3? (No)
     o What are the possible remainders when a number is divided by 3? (0, 1, or 2)
     o Look at the circled numbers. All of them are divisible by 3. The remainder is 0 when they are divided by 3.
     o What happens if you add the digits of a circled number? (Give an example. The sum of the digits for 54 is 9.)
     o Add the digits of some more of the circled numbers. Do you see a pattern? Try adding the digits of 96. (9 + 6 = 15) Now add the digits again. (1 + 5 = 6). Is this divisible by 3? (yes) Is 96? (yes)
     o Try adding the digits of the numbers that are not circled. Is the sum of the digits divisible by 3? (no)
     o Does this rule work with 3-digit numbers? Try and see. (yes)
     (Note: Some students may wonder why this divisibility test works for 3's. You can offer the following explanation illustrating with number discs. A 3-digit number can be divided up into 99's, 9's, and remaining ones. All the 99's and 9's are divisible by 3. If the sum of the remaining ones is divisible by 3, then the whole number is — there will be no remainders.

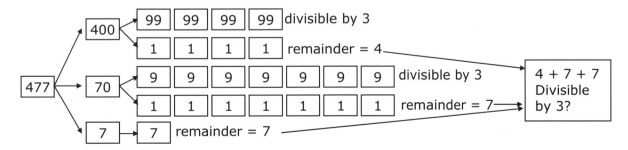

- Now have students cover up the numbers on their boards that they land on when counting up by 4's.
  - What is the remainder if a circled number is divided by 4? (0)
  - Divide some other numbers by 4. What are the possible remainders? (1, 2, or 3)
  - Do you see a pattern with the circled numbers? (They are even)
  - So a number that can be divided by 4 without leaving a remainder can also be divided by 2. Are all numbers that are divisible by 2 also divisible by 4? (No)
  - There isn't an easy way to tell if any even number is divisible by 4 as there is with 3's. (You may want to tell them that if they know the last 2 digits of a number are divisible by 4, then the whole number is divisible by 4, and let them investigate with some 3-digit numbers. 324 is divisible by 4, since 24 is. Divisibility rules will be looked at again in *Primary Mathematics 4A*.)
- Now have students cover up the numbers on their boards that they land on when counting up by 5's. Follow a similar procedure to show that the remainder of a number divided by 5 can be 0, 1, 2, 3, or 4. Numbers that end in 5 or 0 are divisible by 5.

Review

Objectives

- Review previous topics

Suggested number of sessions: 2

	Objectives	Textbook	Workbook	Activities
46 47	▪ Review	p. 67, Review A	Review 3	R.1

Activity R.1   **Review**

1. Have students do **Review A, textbook p. 67.**
   - Students can solve problems individually and then some of them can present their solutions. Students must determine which operation(s) they need to solve the word problems. Help them model the problems if that helps with the solution. For example:
     #10

     Sulin's money = 1 unit = $240
     Meifin's money = 3 units = $240 x 3 = $720
     Total money = $240 + $720 = $960
     Or: Total money = 4 units = $240 x 4 = $960
     They have $960 altogether.

2. Provide additional review in the form of games or worksheets or additional word problems.

3. **Game**:
   - Divide students into groups. Provide each group with number discs in a sack (1's, 10's, and 100's) and a number cube labeled with 2, 3, 3, 4, 4, and 5.
   - Each student takes out ten number discs without looking at them before taking them out of the bag. They use them to form a 3-digit number. They write the number down. Then, they throw the cube.
     - Game 1: The students divide the number formed from the discs by the number on the cube. After a specified number of rounds, the students add up their remainders. The one with the highest (or smallest) remainder wins.
     - Game 2: The students multiply the number formed from the discs by the number on the cube. The one with the highest (or lowest) product gets a point. The one with the most points after a specified number of rounds wins.

Workbook Review 3

Unit 4 – Multiplication Tables of 6, 7, 8 and 9

Objectives for the unit:
• Learn the multiplication and division facts for 6, 7, 8, and 9.
• Multiply numbers up to 1000 by 6, 7, 8, or 9.
• Divide numbers up to 1000 by 6, 7, 8, or 9.

Suggested number of sessions: 20

	Objectives	Textbook	Workbook	Activities
Part 1 : Looking Back				**1 session**
48	▪ Review facts for multiplication and division by 2, 3, 4, 5, and 10. ▪ Double numbers within 100 mentally.	pp. 68-69	Ex. 28	4.1a
Part 2 : Multiplying and Dividing by 6				**5 sessions**
49	▪ Determine new facts for multiplication by 6 from known facts. ▪ Learn facts for multiplication by 6 (four new facts).	pp. 71-73, tasks 1-3	Ex. 29	4.2a
50	▪ Relate division by 6 to multiplication by 6. ▪ Learn facts for division by 6.	p.70 p. 73, task 4	Ex. 30	4.2b
51	▪ Multiply numbers within 1000 by 6.	p. 74, tasks 5-6	Ex. 31	4.2c
52	▪ Divide numbers within 1000 by 6.	p. 74, tasks 7-8	Ex. 32	4.2d
53	▪ Practice.	p. 75, Practice 4A	Ex. 33	4.2e
Part 3 : Multiplying and Dividing by 7				**5 sessions**
54	▪ Determine new facts for multiplication by 7 from known facts. ▪ Learn facts for multiplication by 7 (three new facts).	p. 76 pp. 77-79, tasks 1-4	Ex. 34	4.3a
	▪ Learn facts for division by 7.	p. 79, task 5		
55	▪ Multiply numbers within 1000 by 7.	p. 79, task 6	Ex. 35	4.3b
56	▪ Divide numbers within 1000 by 7.	p. 79, tasks 7-8	Ex. 36	4.3c
57	▪ Practice.	p. 80, Practice 4B	Ex. 37	4.3d
58	▪ Practice.	p. 81, Practice 4C	Review 4	

	Objectives	Textbook	Workbook	Activities
Part 4 : Multiplying and Dividing by 8				**4 sessions**
59	▪ Determine new facts for multiplication by 8 from known facts and doubling. ▪ Learn facts for multiplication by 8 (two new facts).	p. 82 p. 83, tasks 1-2	Ex. 38	4.4a
	▪ Learn facts for division by 8.	p. 83, task 3		
60	▪ Multiply numbers within 1000 by 8.	p. 83, task 4	Ex. 39	4.4b
61	▪ Divide numbers within 1000 by 8.	p. 83, task 5	Ex. 40	4.4c
62	▪ Practice.	p. 84, Practice 4D p. 85, Practice 4E	Ex. 41	4.4d
Part 5 : Multiplying and Dividing by 9				**5 sessions**
63	▪ Determine new facts for multiplication by 9 from known facts. ▪ Learn facts for multiplication by 9 (one new fact).	p. 86 pp. 87-88, tasks 1-4	Ex. 42	4.5a
	▪ Learn facts for division by 9.	p. 88, task 5		
64	▪ Multiply numbers within 1000 by 9.	p. 88, task 6	Ex. 43	4.5b
65	▪ Divide numbers within 1000 by 9.	p. 88, task 7	Ex. 44	4.5c
66	▪ Practice.	p. 89, Practice 4F	Ex. 45	4.5d
67	▪ Practice.	p. 90, Practice 4G		

Part 1: Looking Back (pp. 68-69)   1 session

Objectives

- Review multiplication and division by 2, 3, 4, 5, and 10.

Materials

- Blank multiplication chart
- Filled in multiplication chart
- Blank multiplication charts for students
- Number cards 1-9, 4 sets per group

Homework

- Workbook Exercise 28

Notes

Students should know the multiplication and division facts for 2, 3, 4, 5 and 10 by now. They are briefly reviewed in this section.

Students learned in *Primary Mathematics 2* that they can double a number (5 + 5) to find 2 times that number (5 x 2 or 2 x 5). They can double the product of 2 times a number to get 4 times that number (double the double). In this unit, they will learn that they can double the product of 4 times a number to get 8 times that number and the product of 3 times a number to get 6 times a number. For example, if they know 3 x 6 is 18, they can double 18 to get 6 x 6. Doubling a number involves mental math. In doubling 18, they have to mentally double the 10 to get 20, double the 8 to get 16, and then add 20 and 16 [18 x 2 = (10 x 2) + (8 x 2)]. This process can be extended for more capable students to mental multiplication of any 2-digit number by a 1-digit number. For example: 39 x 5 = 150 + 45 = 195.

As the students go through the sections for multiplying and dividing by 6, 7, 8, and 9, they can practice the math facts with games or other fact practice.

Activity 4.1a   **Doubles**

1. Review multiplication facts for 2, 3, 4, 5, and 10.
    *   Have students fill in a multiplication chart
        with the facts they have already learned, if
        they have not yet done so. Help them fill in
        the squares for the last 16 facts. Tell them
        that they are going to learn these last facts.
        Draw a diagonal through the square and
        point out that since a fact such as 4 x 5 is
        the same as 5 x 4, they really only need to
        learn the facts on one side of the diagonal
        and along the diagonal, which is a number
        times itself. So they only need to learn 16
        new facts to know all the facts up to 10 x
        10.

x	1	2	3	4	5	6	7	8	9	10
1	1	2	3	4	5	6	7	8	9	10
2	2	4	6	8	10	12	14	16	18	20
3	3	6	9	12	15	18	21	24	27	30
4	4	8	12	16	20	24	28	32	36	40
5	5	10	15	20	25	30	35	40	45	50
6	6	12	18	24	30	36	42	48	46	60
7	7	14	21	28	35	42	49	56	63	70
8	8	16	24	32	40	48	56	64	72	80
9	9	18	27	36	45	56	63	72	81	90
10	10	20	30	40	50	60	70	80	90	100

2. Double 2-digit numbers mentally.
    *   Display a completed multiplication chart. Point to the top row and the x2 row. Point out
        that each number in the x2 row is double the number which is above it in the top row.
        Now point to or highlight the x2 row and the x4 row. Ask students if they see a pattern.
        Each number in the x4 row is double the number above it in the x2 row. Repeat for the
        x4 and x8 rows. Ask them if they see any other rows where one row is double the
        numbers in another row in the same column. The numbers in the x6 row are double
        those above them in the x3 row, and the numbers in the x10 row are double those in
        the x5 row.
    *   Ask students to double, or multiply by 2, some 2-digit numbers where renaming does
        not occur. Point out they are doubling the tens and the ones and then adding:

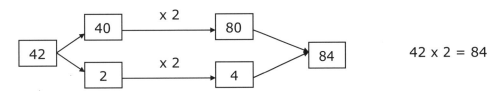

42 x 2 = 84

    *   Now have them double some 2-digit numbers where renaming occurs. They can double
        the value of each digit mentally, and add the products mentally. You can illustrate with
        number bonds:

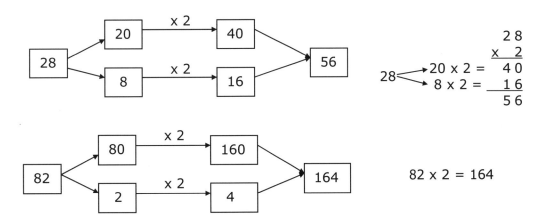

$$\begin{array}{r} 28 \\ \times\ 2 \end{array}$$
28 → 20 x 2 = 40
    → 8 x 2 = 16
          56

82 x 2 = 164

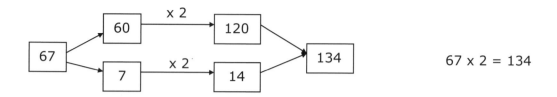

67 x 2 = 134

- Give students additional 2-digit numbers to practice multiplying by 2 (doubling) mentally.
- If the class has difficulty with problems where both the tens and ones are regrouped, limit the problems to ones where regrouping occurs only once, or only to doubling numbers less than 50. You may need to continue this in the next class so that, after this is mastered, you can go on to doubling numbers where both tens and ones are regrouped.

3. (Optional) Multiply a 2-digit number by 3, 4, or 5 mentally.
- Extend doubling 2-digit numbers mentally to multiplying 2-digit numbers by 3, 4, and 5 mentally. Depending on the abilities of your class, you can limit practice to easier numbers. Students should be able to choose methods. Some might multiply all 2-digit numbers mentally; others may prefer only to multiply easy ones mentally and use the multiplication algorithm for harder ones. Students should be allowed to choose the approach they feel most comfortable with, and may gradually use more mental computation later.
- Show the process using number bonds:

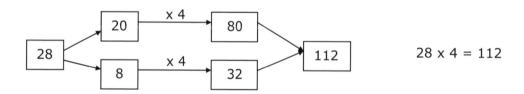

28 x 4 = 112

- You can also show the process as in the following examples:

```
32 x 3      30  +  2           52 x 4      50  +  2
            x       3                      x       4
            90  +  6  = 96                 200 + 8  = 208

47 x 3      40  +  7           39 x 5      30  +  9
            x       3                      x       5
            120 + 21 = 141                 150 + 45 = 195
```

- US: Since there are 12 inches in a foot, and 12 hours around the clock, it is particularly useful to be able to mentally multiply by 12. Ask students to mentally multiply 12 by 2, 3, 4, and 5.
- Have students do the Mental Math worksheet on the following page.
- Students can also do any of the games in the previous unit by finding the answers using mental math.

Workbook Exercise 28

Mental Math 9

1.   77 x 3 = 210 + 21 = _____

2.   34 x 5 = _____ + _____ = _____

3.   87 x 2 = _____ + _____ = _____

4.   43 x 4 = _____ + _____ = _____

5.   45 x 3 = _____ + _____ = _____

6.   85 x 5 = _____

7.   62 x 2 = _____

8.   33 x 5 = _____

9.   43 x 3 = _____

10. 63 x 4 = _____

11. 23 x 2 = _____

12. 56 x 3 = _____

13. 36 x 5 = _____

14. 71 x 2 = _____

15. 21 x 4 = _____

16. 64 x 5 = _____

17. 47 x 3 = _____

18. 31 x 4 = _____

19. 69 x 2 = _____

20. 28 x 3 = _____

21. 82 x 5 = _____

22. 49 x 4 = _____

23. 36 x 2 = _____

24. 83 x 3 = _____

25. 27 x 5 = _____

Part 2: Multiplying and Dividing by 6 (pp. 70-75)	5 sessions

Objectives

- Learn the facts for multiplication and division by 6.
- Multiply and divide numbers within 1000 by 6.

Materials

- Centimeter graph paper
- Ten equal strips of 6 joined squares that can be displayed
- Number cards 1-10, 4 sets per group
- Number cube labeled with 2, 3, 4, 5, 6, and 6
- Hundreds charts for students
- 20 cards per group, 10 with division facts for 6 (e.g., $36 \div 6$) and 10 with the answers (e.g., 6)

Homework

- Workbook Exercise 29
- Workbook Exercise 30
- Workbook Exercise 31
- Workbook Exercise 32
- Workbook Exercise 33

Notes

Students will be learning the facts for multiplication and division by 6 in this section. Until the facts are memorized, they can use various methods for computing unknown facts from known facts:

Add 6 to the fact for one less.	$6 \times 5 = 30$ $6 \times 6 = 30 + 6 = 36$
Split the problem into two known problems.	$6 \times 7 = 6 \times 5$ and 6×2 $6 \times 7 = 30 + 12 = 42$
Double the product of the number times 3 to get the number times 6	$7 \times 6 = 7 \times 3 \times 2$ $7 \times 6 = 21 \times 2 = 42$
6×8 can be found by doubling the 6×4, or doubling the 6 three times successively.	$6 \times 8 = 6 \times 4 \times 2 = 24 \times 2 = 48$ 6×8: double 6 three times: 6, 12, 24, 48
6×9 can be found by subtracting 6 from 6×10.	$6 \times 10 = 60$ $6 \times 9 = 60 - 6 = 54$

Centimeter Graph Paper

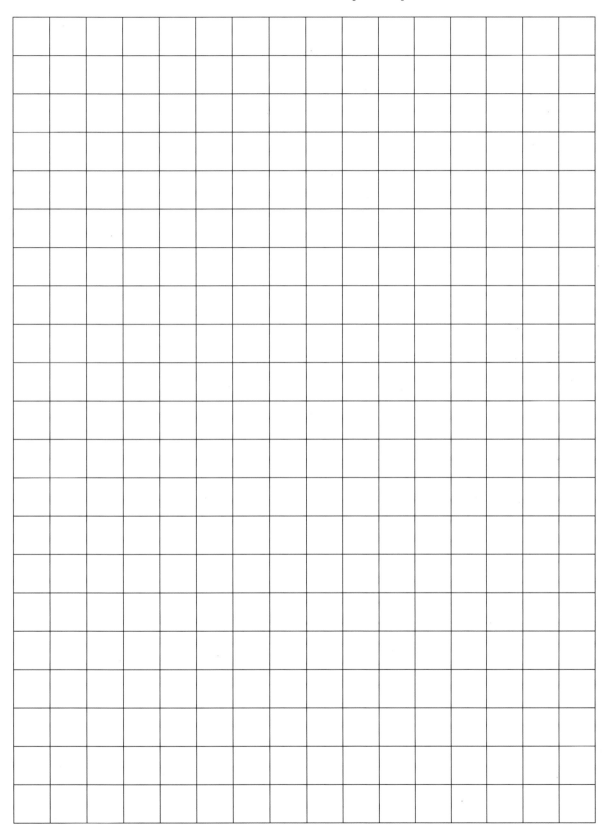

Mental Math 10

1. $3 \times 6 =$ _____

2. $10 \times 6 =$ _____

3. $6 \times 6 =$ _____

4. $9 \times 6 =$ _____

5. $6 \times 8 =$ _____

6. $3 \times 4 =$ _____

7. $5 \times 6 =$ _____

8. $5 \times 4 =$ _____

9. $6 \times 7 =$ _____

10. $8 \times 4 =$ _____

11. $4 \times 6 =$ _____

12. $6 \times 0 =$ _____

13. $7 \times 3 =$ _____

14. $6 \times 9 =$ _____

15. $7 \times 6 =$ _____

16. $36 \div 6 =$ _____

17. $48 \div 6 =$ _____

18. $30 \div 5 =$ _____

19. $6 \div 6 =$ _____

20. $18 \div 6 =$ _____

21. $24 \div 6 =$ _____

22. $42 \div 6 =$ _____

23. $30 \div 6 =$ _____

24. $54 \div 6 =$ _____

25. $28 \div 4 =$ _____

26. $60 \div 6 =$ _____

27. $24 \div 6 =$ _____

28. $35 \div 5 =$ _____

29. $27 \div 3 =$ _____

30. $54 \div 6 =$ _____

Activity 4.2a   **Multiply by 6**

1. Learn facts for multiplication by 6.
   - Give students some centimeter graph paper and have them color in 10 rows of 6.
   - Have students write the equations as shown here. They can look at **task 3, textbook p. 73.**
   - They should realize that each fact is 6 more than the one before, and 6 less than the one after. Point out that they will be learning 4 new facts.
   - Have students practice counting by 6's.
   - Use **tasks 1-2, textbook pp. 71-72,** to discuss methods for finding some of the multiplication facts. Illustrate with strips of 6 squares so you can add or remove 6's.

1 x 6 = 6	6 x 1 = 6
2 x 6 = 12	6 x 2 = 12
3 x 6 = 18	6 x 3 = 18
4 x 6 = 24	6 x 4 = 24
5 x 6 = 30	6 x 5 = 30
6 x 6 = 36	**6 x 6 = 36**
7 x 6 = 42	**6 x 7 = 42**
8 x 6 = 48	**6 x 8 = 48**
9 x 6 = 54	**6 x 9 = 54**
10 x 6 = 60	6 x 10 = 60

Task 1(a)   4 x 6 can be found by doubling 6, and then doubling again: 6, 12, 24.

Task 1(b)   5 x 6 and 6 x 5 can be found by counting by 5's: 5, 10, 15, 20, 25, 30. You can point out that an odd number times 5 gives a product that ends with 5, whereas an even number times 5 gives a product that ends with 0. For 5 x an even number, the ten is half the even number. Half of 6 is 3, so the product of 5 and 6 is 30. For students that are competent with dividing by 2 mentally, you can point out that 5 x any number is 10 x the number divided by 2. 10 x 6 = 60, 60 ÷ 2 = 30, so 5 x 6 = 30.

Task 2(a)   6 x 6 is 6 more than 6 x 5.
             6 x 5 = 30
             6 x 6 = 30 + 6 = 36

Task 2(b)   Split 6 x 7 into 2 products.

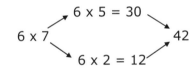

They can also split it differently, such as 6 x 3 and 6 x 4. Let them try this. It is easier to add 12 to 30 than to add 18 and 24.

You can ask students to find 6 x 6 by splitting into two parts other than 6 x 5 and 6 x 1. Some students might suggest 6 x 3 and 6 x 3. Point out that they are doubling 6 x 3 to get 6 x 6. They can try this with the other facts:

6 x 6 = double 3 x 6 = double 18 = 36
7 x 6 = double 3 x 7 = double 21 = 42
8 x 6 = double 3 x 8 = double 24 = 48
9 x 6 = double 3 x 9 = double 27 = 54

Task 2(c)   6 x 8 can also be split into two parts. Students can try different combinations. It is easiest to split it into 6 x 4 and 6 x 4 and double 24.

Put down one strip of 6. Ask them to double it. That gives 6 x 2. Ask them to double it again. That gives 6 x 4. Ask them to double it a third time. That gives 6 x 8. Tell them they can find 6 x 8 by doubling 6 three times: 6, 12, 24, 48. (Other methods for finding 6 x 8 by adding 8 to 5 x 8 will be given in a later section.)

Task 2(d)   Display 10 strips of 6. Ask for the total. Write 6 x 10 = 60. Remove 1 strip of 6. Ask students to subtract to find the new total. 60 – 6 = 54. This is the same as 6 x 9.

- Provide opportunities for students to practice the facts, particularly the new ones.

2. Game.
   - Divide students into groups of 4. Provide each group with 4 sets of number cards 1-10 and a number cube labeled with 2, 3, 4, 5, 6 and 6. Cards are shuffled and all are dealt.
   - Students each turn over a card and take turns throwing the number cube. They multiply the number on the card with the number on the cube. The student with the highest product gets all the cards and puts them in a separate pile. The student with the most cards after all have been turned over wins.

Workbook Exercise 29

Activity 4.2b   **Divide by 6**

1. Learn facts for division by 6.
   - Write a division equation such as 42 ÷ 6. Remind students that they can answer this by thinking of the number times 6 that equals 42.
   - Discuss **textbook p. 70** and **task 4, textbook p. 73**.
   - Have students write all the facts for division by 6. They can make a table such as the one shown here.
   - Use Mental Math 10 for more practice, now or later.

$42 \div 6 =$ _____   _____ $\times 6 = 42$

1		6	6 ÷ 6 = 1
2		12	12 ÷ 6 = 2
3	x 6	18	18 ÷ 6 = 3
4	⟶	24	24 ÷ 6 = 4
5		30	30 ÷ 6 = 5
6		36	36 ÷ 6 = 6
7	÷ 6	42	42 ÷ 6 = 7
8	⟵	48	48 ÷ 6 = 8
9		54	54 ÷ 6 = 9
10		60	60 ÷ 6 = 10

2. Game
   - Divide students into groups of 4. Give each group 20 cards, 10 with the division facts for 6 without the answer, and 10 with answers.
     o Game 1: Shuffle cards and put them in a 4 by 5 array face down. Each student takes turns turning over 2 cards. If they turn over a pair where one card is the answer to the division fact on the other card, they keep the cards. Otherwise they turn them face down and the next student has a turn. When all of the cards have been taken the student with the most cards wins.
     o Game 2: Stack all the answers face up in the middle. One player is the dealer for each round. The dealer shows one fact card at a time. The student who gets the correct answer first gets the card from the middle. After all the fact cards are turned over, the student with the most cards is the next dealer.

Workbook Exercise 30

Activity 4.2c — Multiply by 6

1. Multiply a 2-digit or 3-digit number by 6.
   - Use the example in the **task 5, textbook p. 74,** to review the steps for the multiplication algorithm. Illustrate with number discs or base-10 blocks if necessary. The steps are the same as learned in Part 3 of Unit 3. Step through some other examples as well.
   - Have students solve the problems in the **task 6, text p. 74**.

2. Practice.
   - Divide students into groups. Give each group four sets of number cards 0-9, shuffled. For each round, a player draws 3 cards and forms a 3-digit number. All the players multiply it by 6. They then compare answers. If any player gets a different answer, they must determine where the error is.

Workbook Exercise 31

Activity 4.2d — Divide by 6

1. Divide a 2-digit or 3-digit number by 6.
   - Use the example in the **task 7, textbook p. 74,** to review the steps for the division algorithm. Illustrate with number discs or base-10 blocks if necessary. Step through some other examples as well.
   - Have the students solve the problems in the **task 8, textbook p. 74**.
   - Provide the students with more problems for practice.

2. Investigate divisibility by 6 and remainders.
   - Give students copies of a hundreds chart. Have them circle the numbers they land on when counting by 6's. Ask them if they see any patterns. For example, each number is one space down and four back from the previous number. Each second number is one down and two to the right.
   - Ask students to also mark any numbers they land on when they count by 3 with an X that are not already marked. They should notice that the circled numbers are also part of the 3's.
   - Ask them if they remember how to tell if a number can be divided by 3 with no remainders. (The sum of the digits is divisible by 3.)
   - Ask if they can see a difference between the numbers X'd and the numbers circled. The circled numbers are all even, whereas those only X'd are odd.
   - Ask them if they can come up with a rule that will tell them whether a number can be divided by 6 without a remainder. The sum of the digits must be divisible by 3, and it must be an even number.
   - Have the students look at some of the problems they solved from the text or the workbook to see if the rule works for 3-digit numbers as well.

1	2	~~3~~	4	5	⑥	7	8	~~9~~	10
11	⑫	13	14	~~15~~	16	17	⑱	19	20
~~21~~	22	23	㉔	25	26	~~27~~	28	29	㉚
31	32	~~33~~	34	35	㊱	37	38	~~39~~	40
41	㊷	43	44	~~45~~	46	47	㊽	49	50
~~51~~	52	53	(54)	55	56	~~57~~	58	59	(60)
61	62	~~63~~	64	65	(66)	67	68	~~69~~	70
71	(72)	73	74	~~75~~	76	77	(78)	79	80
~~81~~	82	83	(84)	85	86	~~87~~	88	89	(90)
91	92	~~93~~	94	95	(96)	97	~~98~~	99	100

- Point to some numbers between the circled numbers and ask the student to divide them by 6. Ask them for all the possible remainders for a number divided by 6. They are 0, 1, 2, 3, 4, or 5.

3. Game.
   - Divide students into teams. Give all the teams a problem involving division of a 2-digit or 3-digit number by 6. The team gets a point if they get the correct answer first. If they get an incorrect answer, they lose a point, and the team that finds the error gets the point.

Workbook Exercise 32

Activity 4.2e   **Practice**

1. Use **Practice 4A, textbook p. 75**.
   - You can require students to draw a diagram for the word problems.
   - Students can solve the problems individually and then discuss their solutions.

Workbook Exercise 33

| **Part 3: Multiplying and Dividing by 7 (pp. 76-81)** | **5 sessions** |

Objectives

* Learn the facts for multiplication and division by 7.
* Multiply and divide numbers within 1000 by 7.

Materials

* Centimeter graph paper
* Strips of 7 items that can be displayed
* Number cards 1-10, 4 sets per group
* Number cubes labeled with 3, 4, 6, 6, 7, and 7
* Hundreds charts for students
* 30 cards per group, 10 with division facts for 7 (e.g., 49 ÷ 7), 10 with the answers (e.g., 7), 5 with multiplication facts 6 x 7, 7 x 7, 7 x 8, 7 x 9, and 6 x 8, and 5 with those answers

Homework

* Workbook Exercise 34
* Workbook Exercise 35
* Workbook Exercise 36
* Workbook Exercise 37

Notes

Students will be learning the facts for multiplication and division by 7 in this section. Until the facts are memorized, they can use various methods for computing unknown facts from known facts, such as:

Add 7 to the fact for one less.	7 x 5 = 35 7 x 6 = 35 + 7 = 42
Split the problem into two known problems.	7 x 7 = 7 x 5 and 7 x 2 7 x 7 = 35 + 14 = 49
7 x 8 can be found by doubling the 7 x 4, or doubling 7 three times successively.	7 x 8 = 7 x 4 x 2 = 28 x 2 = 56 7 x 8: double 7 three times: 7, 14, 28, 56
7 x 9 can be found by subtracting 7 from 7 x 10	7 x 10 = 70 7 x 9 = 70 - 7 = 63

Mental Math 11

1. $6 \times 7 = $ _____

2. $9 \times 7 = $ _____

3. $9 \times 6 = $ _____

4. $7 \times 8 = $ _____

5. $7 \times 5 = $ _____

6. $8 \times 7 = $ _____

7. $7 \times 6 = $ _____

8. $4 \times 7 = $ _____

9. $6 \times 6 = $ _____

10. $5 \times 7 = $ _____

11. $7 \times 9 = $ _____

12. $6 \times 8 = $ _____

13. $7 \times 7 = $ _____

14. $49 \times 7 = $ _____

15. $78 \times 7 = $ _____

16. $56 \div 7 = $ _____

17. $42 \div 7 = $ _____

18. $48 \div 6 = $ _____

19. $49 \div 7 = $ _____

20. $28 \div 7 = $ _____

21. $14 \div 7 = $ _____

22. $7 \div 7 = $ _____

23. $21 \div 7 = $ _____

24. $35 \div 7 = $ _____

25. $42 \div 7 = $ _____

26. $42 \div 6 = $ _____

27. $54 \div 6 = $ _____

28. $35 \div 7 = $ _____

29. $63 \div 7 = $ _____

30. $49 \div 7 = $ _____

Activity 4.3a   **Multiply and divide by 7**

1. Learn facts for multiplication by 7.
   - Give students some centimeter graph paper and have them color in 10 rows of 6.
   - Have students write the equations as shown here. They can look at the **task 4, textbook p. 79.**
   - Point out that they will be learning 3 new facts.
   - Have students practice counting by 7's.
   - Discuss **textbook p. 76**.
   - Use **tasks 1-2, textbook pp. 77-78,** to discuss methods of finding some of the multiplication facts. Illustrate with overhead strips of 7 so you can add or remove 7's.

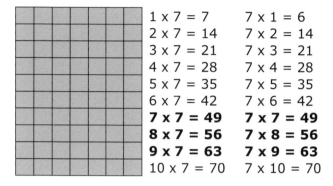

1 x 7 = 7	7 x 1 = 6
2 x 7 = 14	7 x 2 = 14
3 x 7 = 21	7 x 3 = 21
4 x 7 = 28	7 x 4 = 28
5 x 7 = 35	7 x 5 = 35
6 x 7 = 42	7 x 6 = 42
7 x 7 = 49	**7 x 7 = 49**
8 x 7 = 56	**7 x 8 = 56**
9 x 7 = 63	**7 x 9 = 63**
10 x 7 = 70	7 x 10 = 70

    Task 1   Students should already know 3 x 7 and 5 x 7. They can count by 3's to find 3 x 7, rather than 7's. They can count by 5's to find 5 x 7. Counting by 5's is easier than counting by 7's.

    Task 2(a)   7 x 6 is 7 more than 7 x 5.

                 7 x 5 = 35

                 7 x 6 = 35 + 7 = 42

    Task 2(b)   Split 6 x 7 into two products.

                 They can also split it differently, such as 7 x 3 and 7 x 4. Let them try this. It might be easier to add 21 to 28 than to add 35 and 14.

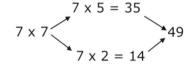

    Task 2(c)   7 x 8 can also be split into two parts. Students can try different combinations. It is easiest to split it into 7 x 4 and 7 x 4, so they can double 28.

                 Put down one strip of 7. Ask them to double it. That gives 7 x 2. Ask them to double it again. That gives 7 x 4. Ask them to double it a third time, giving 7 x 8. Tell them they can find 7 x 8 by doubling 7 three times: 7, 14, 28, 56.

    Task 2(d)   Display 10 strips of 7. Ask for the total. Write 7 x 10 = 70. Remove 1 strip of 7. Ask students to subtract to find the new total. 70 – 7 = 63. This is the same as 6 x 9.

   - Discuss **task 3, textbook p. 78**. Also ask how many days are in 3, 9, 5, 6, 7, or 8 weeks.

2. Learn facts for division by 7.
   - Write a division equation such as $42 \div 7$. Remind students that they can answer this by thinking of the number times 7 that equals 42.
   - Have students write facts for the division by 7. They can make a table like the one here.
   - Discuss **task 5, textbook p. 79**.
   - Ask students for the number of weeks in 63 days? 35 days? etc.
   - You can use the Mental Math 11 for more practice.

$42 \div 7 = \underline{\quad}$ $\underline{\quad} \times 7 = 42$

1		7	$7 \div 7 = 1$
2		14	$14 \div 7 = 2$
3	x 7	21	$21 \div 7 = 3$
4	$\longrightarrow$	28	$28 \div 7 = 4$
5		35	$35 \div 7 = 5$
6		42	$42 \div 7 = 6$
7	$\div 7$	49	$49 \div 7 = 7$
8	$\longleftarrow$	56	$56 \div 7 = 8$
9		63	$63 \div 6 = 9$
10		70	$70 \div 7 = 10$

Workbook Exercise 34

Activity 4.3b   **Multiply by 7**

1. Multiply a 2-digit or 3-digit number by 7.
   - Have students solve the problems in the **task 6, textbook p. 79**.
   - They can also do **problems 1-3, Practice 4B, textbook p. 80**.

2. Game
   - Divide students into groups of 4. Give each group 30 index cards with division or multiplication facts on 15 of them and answers on 15 of them (see materials list).
     o Game 1: Shuffle cards and place face down in a 6 x 5 array. Each student takes turns turning over 2 cards. If they turn over a pair, (where one card is the answer to a division fact on the other card) they keep the cards. Otherwise they turn them face down and the next student has a turn. When all of the cards have been taken the student with the most cards wins. For a longer game, they can include their cards from the previous game for division by 6.
     o Game 2: Place all the answers face up in the middle. One player is the dealer for each round. The dealer shows one fact card at a time. The student who gets the correct answer first gets the cards from the middle. After all the fact cards are turned over, the student with the most answer cards is the next dealer.

Workbook Exercise 35

Activity 4.3c   **Divide by 7**

1. Divide a 2-digit or 3-digit number by 7.
   - Have students solve the problems in the **tasks 7-8, textbook p. 74** and **problem 4, textbook p. 80**.

2. Investigate divisibility by 7 and remainders.
   - Give each student a hundreds chart. Have them circle the numbers they land on when counting by 7's. Ask them if they see any patterns. For example, each number is one row down and three columns back from the previous number. Some of the numbers are even and some are odd.

1	2	3	4	5	6	(7)	8	9	10
11	12	13	(14)	15	16	17	18	19	20
(21)	22	23	24	25	26	27	(28)	29	30
31	32	33	34	(35)	36	37	38	39	40
41	(42)	43	44	45	46	47	48	(49)	50
51	52	53	54	55	(56)	57	58	59	60
61	62	(63)	64	65	66	67	68	69	(70)
71	72	73	74	75	76	(77)	78	79	80
81	82	83	(84)	85	86	87	88	89	90
(91)	92	93	94	95	96	97	(98)	99	100

   - Tell students that there isn't an easy rule to determine if the number is divisible by 7 for 2-digit numbers.
   (There is a rule for larger numbers, but do not teach it to your class except as an enrichment for more capable students, and only use numbers above 180 as examples to avoid negative results. To find out if a number is divisible by 7, take the last digit, double it, and subtract the doubled number from the rest of the number. If the result is divisible by 7, then the number is divisible by 7. If you don't know the new number's divisibility, you can apply the rule again. For example, with 203, double the 3 to get 6 and subtract it from 20 to get 14. 14 is divisible by 7, so 203 is.)
   - Ask students for all the possible remainders if a number is divided by 7. They are 0, 1, 2, 3, 4, 5, and 6.

Workbook Exercise 36

Activity 4.3d   **Practice**

1. Use **Practice 4B, textbook p. 80** and **Practice 4C, textbook p. 81**.
   - Students can solve the problems individually and then discuss their solutions. Have them model the problems. For example:
     #11, p. 80
     Cost of T-shirt = 1 unit = $26
     Cost of jacket = 7 units = $26 x 7 = $182
     Cost of both = $26 + $182 = $208
     or: Cost of both = 8 units = $26 x 8 = $208
     The total cost of both is $208

2. Provide other review or fact practice.

Workbook Exercise 37
Workbook Review 4

Part 4: Multiplying and Dividing by 8 (pp. 82-85)   4 sessions

Objectives

- Learn the facts for multiplication and division by 8.
- Multiply and divide numbers within 1000 by 8.

Materials

- Centimeter graph paper
- Strips of 8 that can be displayed
- Number cards 1-10, 4 sets per group
- Number cubes labeled with 6, 6, 7, 7, 8, and 8
- Hundreds charts for students
- Worksheets with problems involving multiplication and division of a number within 1000 by 8

Homework

- Workbook Exercise 38
- Workbook Exercise 39
- Workbook Exercise 40
- Workbook Exercise 41

Notes

Students will be learning the facts for multiplication and division by 8 in this section. There are only two new facts. Until they are memorized, students can use various methods for computing unknown facts from known facts, such as:

8×8 can be found by doubling the product of 8×4, or doubling 8 three times successively.	$8 \times 8 = 8 \times 4 \times 2 = 32 \times 2 = 64$ 8×8: double 8 three times: 8, 16, 32, 64
8×9 can be found by subtracting 8 from 8×10	$8 \times 10 = 80$ $8 \times 9 = 80 - 8 = 72$
From a known fact for 8, count up 10 and back 2 to get the next fact.	$8 \times 5 = 40$ Count up 10 (from 40) and subtract 2: 48 Count up 10 (from 48) and subtract 2: 56 Count up 10 (from 56) and subtract 2: 64 $8 \times 8 = 64$

Mental Math 12

1. 9 x 8 = _____

2. 5 x 8 = _____

3. 8 x 8 = _____

4. 6 x 8 = _____

5. 8 x 5 = _____

6. 4 x 8 = _____

7. 7 x 8 = _____

8. 8 x 8 = _____

9. 7 x 6 = _____

10. 8 x 6 = _____

11. 8 x 7 = _____

12. 6 x 6 = _____

13. 7 x 7 = _____

14. 43 x 8 = _____

15. 82 x 8 = _____

16. 48 ÷ 8 = _____

17. 64 ÷ 8 = _____

18. 72 ÷ 8= _____

19. 40 ÷ 8 = _____

20. 49 ÷ 7 = _____

21. 32 ÷ 8 = _____

22. 36 ÷ 6 = _____

23. 63 ÷ 7 = _____

24. 64 ÷ 8 = _____

25. 56 ÷ 8 = _____

26. 48 ÷ 8 = _____

27. 48 ÷ 6 = _____

28. 24 ÷ 8 = _____

29. 56 ÷ 7 = _____

30. 16 ÷ 8 = _____

Activity 4.4a   **Multiply and divide by 8**

1. Learn facts for multiplication by 8.

    -   Give students some centimeter graph paper and have them color in 10 rows of 8.
    -   Have students write down the facts for multiplication by 8. Each fact is 8 more than the one before, and 8 less than the one after. Point out that they will be learning only 2 new facts.

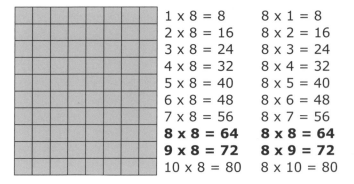

1 x 8 = 8	8 x 1 = 8
2 x 8 = 16	8 x 2 = 16
3 x 8 = 24	8 x 3 = 24
4 x 8 = 32	8 x 4 = 32
5 x 8 = 40	8 x 5 = 40
6 x 8 = 48	8 x 6 = 48
7 x 8 = 56	8 x 7 = 56
8 x 8 = 64	**8 x 8 = 64**
9 x 8 = 72	**8 x 9 = 72**
10 x 8 = 80	8 x 10 = 80

-   Give each student a hundreds chart and have them circle the numbers they land on when counting by 8's. Ask them if they see any patterns. Some possible responses: All the numbers are even. There is one that is 40 more than another one. The next one is down 1 space and back 2 spaces.

1	2	3	4	5	6	7	(8)	9	10
11	12	13	14	15	(16)	17	18	19	20
21	22	23	(24)	25	26	27	28	29	30
31	(32)	33	34	35	36	37	38	39	(40)
41	42	43	44	45	46	47	(48)	49	50
51	52	53	54	55	(56)	57	58	59	60
61	62	63	(64)	65	66	67	68	69	70
71	(72)	73	74	75	76	77	78	79	(80)
81	82	83	84	85	86	87	(88)	89	90
91	92	93	94	95	(96)	97	98	99	100

-   Have students practice counting by 8. Show them they can do this initially by adding 10 and subtracting 2.
-   Discuss **textbook p. 82**. Any number times 8 can be found by doubling that number three times successively. 9 x 8 can be found by subtracting 8 from 10 x 8.
-   Have student provide answers to the problems in **tasks 1-2, textbook p. 83**.

2. Learn facts for division by 8.
    -   Have students write division facts for 8. They can make a table as in the previous activities.
    -   Have the students provide the answers to the problems in the **task 3, textbook p. 83.**
    -   Provide opportunities for students to practice the facts for division by 8, including the Mental Math 12 worksheet and/or adaptations of previous games.

1		8	8 ÷ 8 = 1
2		16	16 ÷ 8 = 2
3	x 8	24	24 ÷ 8 = 3
4	⟶	32	32 ÷ 8 = 4
5		40	40 ÷ 8 = 5
6		48	48 ÷ 8 = 6
7	÷ 8	56	56 ÷ 8 = 7
8	←	64	64 ÷ 8 = 8
9		72	72 ÷ 8 = 9
10		80	80 ÷ 8 = 10

Workbook Exercise 38

Activity 4.3b   **Multiply by 8**

1. Multiply a 2-digit or 3-digit number by 8.
   • Have students solve the problems in the **task 4, textbook p. 83**.
   • You can have students do **problems 1-3, Practice 4D, textbook p. 84**.

Workbook Exercise 39

Activity 4.3c   **Divide by 8**

1. Divide a 2-digit or 3-digit number by 8.
   • Have students solve the problems in **task 5, textbook p. 83**.
   • You can have students do **problems 4-5, Practice 4D, textbook p. 84**.
   • Provide additional practice in dividing a number within 1000 by 8, either through worksheets or games or both.

2. Investigate possible remainders for division by 8.
   • Ask students for all possible remainders when a number is divided by 8. They are 0, 1, 2, 3, 4, 5, 6, and 7. (A number is divisible by 8 if the number formed by the last 3 digits is divisible by 8, but 4-digit numbers are beyond the scope of this level.)

Workbook Exercise 40

Activity 4.3d   **Practice, word problems**

1. Use **Practice 4D, textbook p. 84,** and **Practice 4E, textbook p. 85**.
   • Students can solve the problems individually and then discuss their solutions. Have them model the problem when necessary. For example:
      #10

      $245 $103

      Payment for 1 month = 1 unit = $103
      Payments for 8 months = 8 units = $103 x 8 = $824
      Total cost + $245 + $824 = $1069

2. Provide continued fact practice.

Workbook Exercise 41

| **Part 5: Multiplying and Dividing by 9 (pp. 86-90)** | **5 sessions** |

Objectives

- Learn the facts for multiplication and division by 9.
- Multiply and divide numbers within 1000 by 9.

Materials

- Centimeter graph paper
- Strips of 9 that can be displayed
- Number cards 1-10, 4 sets per group
- Number cube labeled with 6, 7, 8, 8, 9, and 9
- Hundreds charts for students

Homework

- Workbook Exercise 42
- Workbook Exercise 43
- Workbook Exercise 44
- Workbook Exercise 45

Notes

Students will be learning the facts for multiplication and division by 9 in this section. There is only one new fact. Students can use a variety of methods to find the x9 facts.

Use the x10 facts.	$10 \times 9 = 90$ $9 \times 9 = 90 - 9 = 81$
Using their fingers.	This is illustrated on p. 87 of the text.
Subtract 1 from the number being multiplied by 10 to get the tens digit. Find the difference between that and 9 to get the ones digit.	9×7 The tens digit is $7 - 1 = 6$ The ones digit is $9 - 6 = 3$ $9 \times 7 = 63$

Mental Math 13

1. $6 \times 9 =$ _____

2. $7 \times 7 =$ _____

3. $9 \times 9 =$ _____

4. $9 \times 7 =$ _____

5. $8 \times 8 =$ _____

6. $5 \times 9 =$ _____

7. $8 \times 9 =$ _____

8. $9 \times 6 =$ _____

9. $7 \times 9 =$ _____

10. $3 \times 9 =$ _____

11. $4 \times 9 =$ _____

12. $6 \times 6 =$ _____

13. $9 \times 8 =$ _____

14. $62 \times 9 =$ _____

15. $21 \times 9 =$ _____

16. $54 \div 9 =$ _____

17. $81 \div 9 =$ _____

18. $63 \div 9 =$ _____

19. $63 \div 7 =$ _____

20. $72 \div 9 =$ _____

21. $45 \div 9 =$ _____

22. $36 \div 6 =$ _____

23. $48 \div 8 =$ _____

24. $81 \div 9 =$ _____

25. $49 \div 7 =$ _____

26. $27 \div 9 =$ _____

27. $56 \div 8 =$ _____

28. $72 \div 8 =$ _____

29. $36 \div 9 =$ _____

30. $64 \div 8 =$ _____

Activity 4.5a   **Multiply and divide by 9**

1. Learn facts for multiplication by 9.
    *   Provide students with hundreds charts and have them circle the numbers they land on when counting by 9's. Ask them if they see any patterns. Each circled number is down 1 and back 1 from the previous number.

1	2	3	4	5	6	7	8	⑨	10
11	12	13	14	15	16	17	⑱	19	20
21	22	23	24	25	26	㉗	28	29	30
31	32	33	34	35	㊱	37	38	39	40
41	42	43	44	㊺	46	47	48	49	50
51	52	53	�554	55	56	57	58	59	60
61	62	㊳	64	65	66	67	68	69	70
71	㊲	73	74	75	76	77	78	79	80
㊶	82	83	84	85	86	87	88	89	㊐
91	92	93	94	95	96	97	98	㊙	100

*   Have students write the multiplication fact for each circled number. Ask them to look at the answers and describe any patterns they see. Lead them to see that the tens digits increase by 1 and the ones digits decrease by 1.
    o   The sum of the two digits is 9.
    o   The tens digit is one less than the number being multiplied by 9.

When multiplying a 1-digit number by 9, the tens digit of the product will be one less than that number, and the ones digit is the difference between the tens digit and 9.

1 x 9 = 9	9 x 1 = 9
2 x 9 = 18	9 x 2 = 18
3 x 9 = 27	9 x 3 = 27
4 x 9 = 36	9 x 4 = 36
5 x 9 = 45	9 x 5 = 45
6 x 9 = 54	9 x 6 = 54
7 x 9 = 63	9 x 7 = 63
8 x 9 = 72	9 x 8 = 72
9 x 9 = 81	**9 x 9 = 81**
10 x 9 = 90	9 x 10 = 90

*   Have students practice counting by 9's without looking at the list.
*   Discuss **textbook p. 86**. Students should see that the product of a number times 9 can be found by subtracting 9 from the ten of that number. They can look at their hundreds chart and see how many they have to count backwards by from the ten to get to the circled number. For example, in 7 x 9 they can go to 70 to get to 7 x 10, and then they need to go back 7 to get to 63.
*   Discuss **tasks 1-2, textbook p. 87**. Let students practice the method shown in task 2 for finding the product of a number and 9. They hold their hands before them. The first finger on the left is 1, the next 2, and so forth. They bend the finger corresponding to the number being multiplied by 9. The number of fingers to the left of the bent finger is the tens digit, and the number of fingers to the right is the ones digit.
*   Discuss **task 3, textbook p. 88**.
*   Have students do **task 4, textbook p. 88**.

2. Learn facts for division by 9.
    *   Have students write facts for division by 9. They can make a table as in the previous activities.
    *   Students might notice that if the sum of the digits of a 2-digit number is 9, then the quotient when the number is divided by 9 is one more than the tens digit.
    *   Have the students do **task 5, textbook p. 83**.
    *   Provide opportunities for students to practice the facts for division by 9, including the Mental Math 13 worksheet.

1		9	9 ÷ 9 = 1
2		18	18 ÷ 9 = 2
3	x 9	27	27 ÷ 9 = 3
4	⟶	36	36 ÷ 9 = 4
5		45	45 ÷ 9 = 5
6		54	54 ÷ 9 = 6
7	÷ 9	63	63 ÷ 9 = 7
8	⟵	72	72 ÷ 9 = 8
9		81	81 ÷ 9 = 9
10		90	90 ÷ 9 = 10

Workbook Exercise 42

Activity 4.5b   **Multiply by 9**

1. Multiply a 2-digit or 3-digit number by 9.
   - Have students solve the problems in **task 6, textbook p. 88**.

2. Games.
   - Divide students into teams or groups. Provide each team with 4 sets of number cards 0-9.
     - Game 1: Each player draws 3 cards, forms a 2-digit number and a 1-digit number, and finds the product. The player or team with the highest product gets a point.
     - Game 2: Each player draws 4 cards, forms a 3-digit number and a 1-digit number, and finds the product. The player or team with the highest product gets a point.

Workbook Exercise 43

Activity 4.5c   **Divide by 9**

1. Have students do **task 7, text p. 88**.

2. Investigate remainders.
   - Ask students for all possible remainders when a number is divided by 9. They are 0, 1, 2, 3, 4, 5, 6, and 7, and 8. Ask students if they know a way of determining if a number can be divided by 9 without a remainder. From activity 4.5a, they should be able to tell you that if the sum of the digits is 9, it can be divided by 9. Have them try this with some 3-digit numbers. Point out that they can ignore any 9's in the digits and simply add the non-9 digits. Illustrate with some examples. For example: Is 999 divisible by 9? What about 998? How about 918? How about 928? They can ignore the 9 and add 2 and 8 to get 10. So 928 can't be divided by 9 without a remainder. If they do get a remainder of 0, they need to recheck their work to find the error.
   (Note: the test for divisibility by 9 works for the same reason that the test for divisibility by 3 works.)

2. Games.
   - Divide students into teams or groups. Provide all the teams with 4 sets of number cards 0-9.
     - Game 1: Each player draws 3 cards, forms a 2-digit number and a 1-digit number, and divides the 2-digit number by the 1-digit number. The player or team with the lowest quotient, or with no remainder, gets a point.
     - Game 2: Each player draws 4 cards, forms a 3-digit number and a 1-digit number, and divides the 3-digit number by the 1-digit number. The player or team with the lowest quotient, or with no remainder, gets a point.

Workbook Exercise 44

Activity 4.5d   **Practice**

1. Use **Practice 4F, textbook p. 89** and **Practice 4G, textbook p. 90**.
   - Students can solve the problems individually and then discuss their solutions. Have them model the problem when necessary.
   - For #11, if the students have trouble, you can point out that a group of 3 apples costs $2. Help them see that the first step is to find the number of groups of 3 apples.

2. Provide other review or fact practice, such as the Mental Math worksheets on the next three pages.

Workbook Exercise 45

Mental Math 14

1. $8 \times 9 =$ _____

2. $48 \div 8 =$ _____

3. $45 \div 9 =$ _____

4. $9 \times 7 =$ _____

5. $6 \times 8 =$ _____

6. $81 \div 9 =$ _____

7. $6 \times 7 =$ _____

8. $64 \div 8 =$ _____

9. $7 \times 9 =$ _____

10. $9 \times 8 =$ _____

11. $63 \div 7 =$ _____

12. $42 \div 6 =$ _____

13. $63 \div 9 =$ _____

14. $56 \div 7 =$ _____

15. $7 \times 6 =$ _____

16. $42 \div 7 =$ _____

17. $72 \div 9 =$ _____

18. $36 \div 6 =$ _____

19. $54 \div 9 =$ _____

20. $56 \div 8 =$ _____

21. $9 \times 9 =$ _____

22. $40 \div 8 =$ _____

23. $8 \times 8 =$ _____

24. $7 \times 7 =$ _____

25. $6 \times 9 =$ _____

26. $72 \div 8 =$ _____

27. $7 \times 8 =$ _____

28. $49 \div 7 =$ _____

29. $54 \div 6 =$ _____

30. $8 \times 7 =$ _____

Mental Math 15

x	4			2		3		5
6			36					
7							56	
8		72						
9					63			

x	5	7	4	6	2	3	9	8
	40							
		49						
							81	
								48

x	2		3	6	4		9	8
				54				
7						35		
								64
6		42						

Mental Math 16

1. $1000 - 652 =$ _____

2. $435 + 98 =$ _____

3. $81 \div 9 =$ _____

4. $1000 - 258 =$ _____

5. $6 \times 8 =$ _____

6. $328 + 671 =$ _____

7. $3420 - 700 =$ _____

8. $64 \div 8 =$ _____

9. $52 \times 4 =$ _____

10. $438 + 98 =$ _____

11. $800 \times 7 =$ _____

12. $3256 - 96 =$ _____

13. $5200 - 400 =$ _____

14. $56 \div 7 =$ _____

15. $7 \times 60 =$ _____

16. $3216 + 6541 =$ _____

17. $72 \div 9 =$ _____

18. $100 - 56 =$ _____

19. $54 + 45 =$ _____

20. $56 \times 3 =$ _____

21. $90 \times 9 =$ _____

22. $1363 + 80 =$ _____

23. $800 \times 8 =$ _____

24. $4000 - 843 =$ _____

25. $6 \times 90 =$ _____

26. $72 \div 8 =$ _____

27. $71 \times 8 =$ _____

28. $3845 + 702 =$ _____

29. $1000 - 42 =$ _____

30. $500 \times 7 =$ _____

Unit 5 – Money

Objectives for the unit:
- Count sets of bills and coins.
- Recognize, read, and write decimal notation for money.
- Add and subtract money within $100.
- Solve word problems involving addition and subtraction of money.

Suggested number of sessions: 8

	Objectives	Textbook	Workbook	Activities
Part 1 : Dollars and Cents				**3 sessions**
68	▪ Recognize, read, and write the decimal notation for money. ▪ Count money in a set of bills and coins. ▪ Convert dollars and cents to cents, and cents to dollars and cents. ▪ Write amounts of money in words and figures.	p. 91 p. 92, tasks 1-4	Ex. 46	5.1a
69	▪ Make change for $1. ▪ Make change for $10, $20, $50, or $100.	p. 92, task 5 p. 93, Practice 5A		5.1b
70	▪ Practice.			5.1c
Part 2 : Addition				**2 sessions**
71	▪ Add money within $10, using mental math or the addition algorithm.	p. 94 pp. 95-96, tasks 1-5	Ex. 47	5.2a
72	▪ Solve word problems involving the addition of money.	pp. 96-97, tasks 6-8	Ex. 48	5.2b
Part 3 : Subtraction				**4 sessions**
73	▪ Subtract money within $10, using mental math or the subtraction algorithm.	p. 98, pp. 99-100, tasks 1-7		5.3a
74	▪ Subtract money from a multiple of $10 by mentally subtracting from 1000.	p. 100, task 8	Ex. 49	5.3b
75	▪ Solve word problems involving the subtraction of money.	pp. 100-101, tasks 9-11	Ex. 50	5.3c
76	▪ Practice.	p. 102, Practice 5B p. 103, Practice 5C	Ex. 51	5.3d

| **Part 1: Dollars and Cents (pp. 91-93)** | **3 sessions** |

Objectives

- Read and write decimal notation for money.
- Count money in a set of bills and coins.
- Convert dollars and cents to cents.
- Convert cents to dollars and cents.
- Make change for bills up to $100.
- Write amounts of money in words and figures.

Materials

- Play money
- Bills and coins that can be displayed
- "Store cards" – index cards with drawings or pictures of various items with a price of less than $75. Have an equal number of items for each price, from less than $1, $5, $20, $50, or $75.

Homework

- Workbook Exercise 46

Notes

Students learned to count, read, and write money up to $10 in *Primary Mathematics 2A*, to convert from dollars and cents to cents and vice-versa, and to make change for $1, $5, and $10. These concepts are reviewed here and extended to amounts of money up to $100. Students will also write amounts of money up to $10,000 in words.

The concept of decimals has not yet been taught. Decimals will be learned *in Primary Mathematics 4B*. In the meantime, the decimal point should be presented as a dot separating dollars from cents.

In making change for $1 on paper, students can use mental math skills for making 100 learned in *Primary Mathematics 2B*. When answering problems on paper, they can think of 100 as 9 tens and 10 ones and find the difference with 9 for the tens and with 10 for the ones. For example,

$$65¢ + \square = \$1$$

$$
\begin{array}{r}
6 \text{ tens } 5 \text{ ones} \\
+ \underline{\square \text{ tens } \square \text{ ones}} \\
9 \text{ tens } 10 \text{ ones}
\end{array}
$$

9 tens – 6 tens = 3 tens, so the tens digit is 3
10 ones – 5 ones = 5 ones, so the ones digit is 5

$$65¢ + 35¢ = \$1$$

Subtracting cents from a dollar will be used in part 4 in mental math techniques for subtracting money. If students did not learn how to mentally "make 100" with a number less than 100, spend extra time with this concept.

Activity 5.1a   **Dollars and cents**

1. Count money in dollars and cents.
   - Display one quarter and ask students for the amount of money. Repeat with 2, 3, and 4 quarters. Students should be able to easily remember that 2 quarters are 50 cents, 3 quarters are 75 cents, and 4 quarters are $1.
   - Display an amount of money consisting of bills and coins less than $100 where the total amount in coins is less than a dollar.
     - o Discuss strategies for counting the money. Tell them we normally count by larger bills first. Then we count the coins by first counting by 25's for the quarters, then by 10's for dimes, then by 5's for nickels, then by 1's for pennies. We can also combine a quarter and a nickel for 30 cents and then count by 10's for dimes.
     - o Write the total amount in figures, for example $42.31. Remind students that a dot separates the dollars and cents.
     - o Repeat with some other examples, discussing convenient ways to group and count the coins.
     - o Be sure to include some examples where there are less than 10 cents. Students should write $1.04 for a dollar and 4 cents, not $1.4. Tell them that there have to be two digits for the number of cents if there are any cents. If there are no ten cents, they must put in a 0 as a place-holder for tens.
     - o Also include some example where the coins add up to $1. They can write the total amount in the dollar amount only, such as $23, or include the dot and two zeros as place-holders for the cents, $23.00.
   - Discuss **textbook p. 91** and **task 1, textbook p. 92**.

2. Convert dollars and cents to cents, and cents to dollars and cents.
   - Display a dollar bill and ask students for the number of cents in a dollar. Write $1 = 100¢. Remind them that the symbol ¢ means cents. Display other combinations of bills and ask students for the number in cents.
   - Display a dollar bill and some cents and ask students for the number of cents. Write the equations, for example: $1.62 = 162¢.

3. Count and write amounts of money in both figures and words.
   - Display a set of coins where the total amount of money is more than $1 and discuss strategies for counting the coins, such as grouping coins into dollars. Write the amount both in cents and dollars and also in cents, such as 206¢ = $2.06.
   - Ask students for the number of:
     - o Nickels in a dollar
     - o Dimes in a dollar
     - o Quarters in a dollar
     - o Nickels in 3 dollars: Since there are 20 nickels in 1 dollar, there are 20 x 3 nickels in 3 dollars.
     - o Dimes in 10 dollars: Since there are 10 dimes in 1 dollar, there are 10 x 10 dimes in 10 dollars.
     - o Quarters in 4 dollars: Since there are 4 quarters in 1 dollar, there are 4 x 4 quarters in 4 dollars.
   - Tell your students you have 23 quarters.
     - o Ask how much money you have in dollars and cents. Lead them to see that they can divide the number of quarters by 4. The quotient is the number of dollars and the remainder the number of quarters left over.
     - o If the remainder is 1, the answer will have 25¢, if it is 2, the answer will have 50¢, and if it is 3, the answer will have 75¢. 23 ÷ 4 = 5 R 3, so 23 quarters is $5.75. Give a few other examples.

- Tell students you have 42 dimes and ask them for the amount in dollars and cents.
  o Since 10 dimes makes $1, and there are 40 dimes, with 2 left over, the amount is $4.20.
  o Give a few other examples.
- Tell students that you have 55 nickels and ask for the amount of money in dollars and cents.
  o Lead them to see that since there are 20 nickels in a dollar, they can count by 20's to the closest 20. Then they can multiply the remaining number of nickels by 5. 55 nickels = 20 + 20 + 15 nickels = $2.75.
  o Ask them for other ways to find the number of cents in 15 nickels. Since there are 2 nickels in a dime, they can divide by 2. The quotient is the number of tens. If the remainder is 1, there is another 5 cents.
  o Now ask them what they would get if they divided the 55 nickels by 2. They would get 27 r 1. 27 is the number of dimes, and there is 1 nickel left over, so the total money is $2.75.
  o Give a few other examples.
- Discuss **tasks 2-4, textbook p. 92**. Write in words the amounts for task 3 and 4. For example, write "three dollars and forty-five cents" for task 4(c).
- Provide other examples for task 4 including larger amounts but less than $100, such as 3456¢ = $34.56. Call on students to come up to the board and write the amount in dollars and cents, and in words.

4. Additional practice in counting money and writing the amount.
   - Divide students into pairs or groups and provide each group with a sack of play money.
   - Students take turns pulling out a handful of money, counting it, and writing the amounts in numerals and words.
   - One student writes an amount of money less than $100, in dollars and cents, or just in cents, or in words, and the other student counts out the correct amount.

Workbook Exercise 46

Activity 5.1b   **Make change**

1. Make change for bills up to $100.
   - Have a set of coins that you can display ready. Tell students you want to buy something that costs 13¢ and pay for it with $1. Ask how much change you would receive. Discuss ways to make change, illustrating with coins. Students can count up to 15¢ with 2 pennies, then to 25¢ with a dime, then to 50¢, 75¢, and $1 with quarters. Ask how you would make change if you had no dimes or quarters. Repeat with a few other examples.
   - Discuss ways to make change for an amount
     o less than $5 paid for with a $5 bill,
     o less than $10 paid for with a $10 bill,
     o less than $20 paid for with a $20 bill,
     o less than $50 paid with a $50 bill,
     o and less than $100 paid with a $100 bill.
     Illustrate with coins and bills.
   - Discuss **task 5, textbook p. 92**. Tell students that when finding the difference on paper, they aren't counting out coins. So they can do these problems using mental strategies.
     o They can count up by 10's to a number in the 90's and then by 1's to 100.

o   They can find the difference between the tens digit and 9, and then the ones digit and 10. Provide other examples. Spend adequate time with this so that students can easily find the difference between $1 and a number of cents less than $1.

2. Have students do **Practice 5A, textbook p. 93**.

Activity 5.1c   **Practice**

1. Provide experience making change.
    *   Use prepared "store cards" or label items around the classroom with a price. All prices should be less than $75. Have an equal number of items with prices less than $1, $5, $20, $50, or $100.
    *   Have some students be shoppers and some clerks. Give the shoppers several bills of different denominations. They can only buy one item at a time and must get change from the clerk. After they buy several items, have them change roles.
    *   Students can form pairs or groups. Distribute the store cards which are divided up among the members of the group or between the two members of a pair. Provide each student with some money. They take turns buying from each other. You can act as the bank and provide change to the person selling if they need it to make change.

Part 2: Addition (pp. 94-97)   2 sessions

Objectives

- Add money within $100.
- Solve word problems involving the addition of money.

Materials

- Play money
- Bills and coins that can be displayed
- Cards with pictures of items and prices of up to $75, or actual items labeled with their price

Homework

- Workbook Exercise 47
- Workbook Exercise 48

Notes

Students learned various methods for adding money within $10 in *Primary Mathematics 2A*. This section reviews these methods, and extends them to adding money within $100. Methods for mentally adding cents include the following:

Add cents by adding tens and then ones. This can be used when the total cents will be less than $1. We can first add enough ones (from the cents) to bring the amount of money to tens, and then the rest of the ones. The problems in this unit will generally involve numbers that end in 0's or 5's in the cents place.

$$\$38.35 + 37¢$$
$$30¢ \quad 7¢$$
$$\$38.35 \xrightarrow{+30¢} 38.65 \xrightarrow{+7¢} 38.72$$

Make a whole number of dollars. This can be used when it is easy to mentally determine what number needs to be added to one set of money to make 100 cents, and subtract that amount from the cents of the other set of money.

$$\$24.70 + 85¢$$
$$30¢ \quad 55¢$$
$$\$24.70 \xrightarrow{+30¢} \$25.00 \xrightarrow{+55¢} \$25.55$$

Add a whole number of dollars, and subtract the difference. This method can be used when the cents in one set of money is close to 100.

$$\$26.25 + 95¢$$
$$\$26.25 \xrightarrow{+\$1} \$27.25 \xrightarrow{-5¢} \$27.20$$

Use the formal algorithm for addition. Take out the dot (making the money cents only), add the resulting numbers, and then put the dot back in for cents. Students can use the formal algorithm when they cannot solve the problem mentally.

Activity 5.2a   **Add money**

1. Add money within $100 using mental math
    techniques.
    -   Use the problems in **task 1, textbook
        p. 95,** to discuss ways of adding cents
        where the total cents will be $1 or less.
        The example shown here is for 1(c).
        Write the problem and elicit answers
        from the students, asking for their
        solutions. Show how these problems
        can be solved by adding the tens of the
        cents and then the fives. You may want
        to include some additional problems
        using cent amounts where one of the
        numbers ends in some other digit than
        0 or 5. Students can add 5 cents first
        or use other mental techniques.

$38.40 + 35¢

$$\$38.40 \xrightarrow{+30¢} \$38.70 \xrightarrow{+5¢} \$38.75$$

$38.40 + 38¢

$$\$38.40 \xrightarrow{+30¢} \$38.70 \xrightarrow{+5¢} \$38.75 \xrightarrow{+3¢} \$38.78$$

-   Use the problem in **task 2, textbook
    p. 95,** to discuss ways of adding cents
    when the total cents will be more than
    $1. The example shown here is for
    2(c). The technique illustrated here is
    to make a $1 (or 100¢).

$5.65 + 45¢
The difference between 65 and 100 is 35.

$$45¢$$
$$\overset{+35¢}{\swarrow} \quad \overset{+10¢}{\searrow}$$
$$\$5.65 \longrightarrow \$6 \longrightarrow \$6.10$$

$3.25 + 85¢
The difference between 25 and 100 is 75.

$$85¢$$
$$\overset{+75¢}{\swarrow} \quad \overset{+10¢}{\searrow}$$
$$\$3.25 \longrightarrow \$4 \longrightarrow \$4.10$$

-   Discuss an additional method with 2(e)
    where a whole number of dollars is
    added and then the difference of 5¢ is
    subtracted. Give a few more examples,
    using other amounts between 90¢ and
    99¢. Students can choose the method
    they are most comfortable with.

$24.70 + 95¢
95¢ = $1 – 5¢

$$\$24.70 \xrightarrow{+\$1} \$25.70 \xrightarrow{-5¢} \$25.65$$

$24.93 + 70¢
93¢ = $1 – 7¢
We can first add 93¢ to 70¢ and then add
the sum to $24.

$$70¢ \xrightarrow{+\$1} \$1.70 \xrightarrow{-7¢} \$1.63 \xrightarrow{+\$24} \$25.63$$

-   Discuss **textbook p. 94**. Sets of money can be added by first adding the dollars, and
    then the cents, using mental math techniques.
-   Discuss **task 3, textbook p. 95**.

2. Have students do the problems in **task 4, textbook p. 95**.

3. Add money within $100 using the addition algorithm.
   - Discuss the first problem in **task 5, textbook p. 96**. Lead students to see that we can change the money into just cents and add the cents together. Then we change the answer back into dollars and cents.
   - With this in mind, we don't actually have to take out the dot. When we write the problem vertically, we need to put the digits in the columns as if we did.
   - Have students do the rest of this task, rewriting the problems vertically.
   - Ask them under what circumstances they might add using this method rather than mental calculation.

Workbook Exercise 47

Activity 5.2b   **Word problems**

1. Discuss **tasks 6-8, textbook pp. 96-97**.
   - In task 7 a part-whole model is used, since the problem involves two parts, the money he spent and the money he had left. In task 8, a comparison model is used, because we are comparing (finding how much less) the money spend this week to the money spent last week.
   - For task 8, you can also ask students to find the total amount of money John saved.
   - Provide some other word problems for practice. If your class is capable, include a few more challenging ones so that you can discuss different solutions with the class. Only use whole numbers of dollars if multiplication and division are involved. For example:
     o Mrs. Clark bought a toy truck and a toy train for her son Brian. The toy truck cost $6.95 and the toy train cost $4.25 more than the toy truck. How much did she pay for the two toys?
     o Peter and Paul shared $28 evenly. Paul then received an additional $15.50. How much money does he now have?

2. Practice.
   - Use "store cards" or labeled items. Assign some students as buyers and some as clerks. Provide the buyers with a $100 bill and the clerks with money to make change.
   - Students select two or more items to purchase. They must write down the cost of each item and then add the amounts together to find the sum before taking the items to the clerk. The sum has to be less than $100. They tell the clerk the sum and pay him or her. The clerk needs to give them change. They need to verify that the clerk gives them the correct change.

Workbook Exercise 48

| **Part 3: Subtraction (pp. 98–103)** | **4 sessions** |

Objectives

- Subtract money within $100.
- Solve word problems involving the subtraction of money.

Materials

- Play money (e.g., "Giant Classroom Money Kit")
- Bills and coins that can be displayed
- Cards with pictures of items and prices of up to $75, or actual items labeled with their price

Homework

- Workbook Exercise 49
- Workbook Exercise 50
- Workbook Exercise 51

Notes

Students learned various methods for subtracting money within $10 in *Primary Mathematics 2A*. This section reviews these methods, and extends them to subtracting money within $100. Methods for mentally subtracting cents include the following:

Subtract cents by first subtracting tens, then ones. This can be used if there are enough cents to subtract from without renaming a dollar. In subtracting the cents, we can first subtract to get to the ten, then the rest of the cents.

$38.65 – 37¢

$$\$38.65 \xrightarrow{-30¢} 38.35 \xrightarrow{-7¢} 38.28$$

Subtract the cents from one of the dollars. This can be used when it is easy to mentally find the difference with 100 cents.

$24.70 – 85¢

$23.70 $1

$1 – 85¢ = 15¢

$$\$23.70 \xrightarrow{+15¢} \$23.85$$

Subtract a whole number of dollars and add the difference. This method can be used when the money being subtracted is close to 100 cents.

$26.25 – 95¢

$$\$26.25 \xrightarrow{-\$1} \$25.25 \xrightarrow{+5¢} \$25.30$$

Use the formal algorithm for subtraction. Take out the dot (making the money cents only), subtract the numbers, and then put the dot back in for cents. This method can be used when it is not easy to subtract mentally.

To subtract from $10, we can think of $10 as $9 + $1 and then subtract the dollars from $9 and the cents from $1.

$10 – $4.70
$9 $1

$9 – $4 = $5
$1 – 70¢ = 30¢
$10 – $4.70 = $5.30

To subtract from $100, the dollars can be mentally subtracted from $99 and the cents from $1.

$100 – $52.90
$90 $9 $1

$90 – $50 = $40 (think of the difference of 9 and 5 and write it down: $**4**____)
$9 – $2 = $7 (think of the difference between 9 and 2 and write it down: $4**7**__)
$1 – 90¢ = 10¢ (find the difference between $1 and the cents and write the cents down: $47.**10**)
$100 - $52.90 = $47.10

You can discuss these mental techniques with your students during this section. Some students will be more able to apply them than others. Allow students to solve the problems using any of the methods learned, including the subtraction algorithm. Students can also find the answer by imagining how they would make change.

Subtracting money on paper, as taught here, uses different methods than making change, where the money is counted up, first using coins to get to $1, and then bills to get to the amount tendered.

Activity 5.3a   **Subtract money**

1. Subtract money within $100 using mental math techniques.

-   Use the problems in **task 1, textbook p. 99,** to discuss ways of subtracting cents where a dollar does not have to be renamed. The example shown here is for 1(c). Write the problem and elicit answers from the students, asking them for their solutions. Show how these problems can be solved by subtracting the tens and then the fives. Include some additional problems subtracting cent amounts that end in some other number than 0 or 5. Students can subtract the tens, then the fives, then the ones, or use other mental techniques.

    $35.85 – 45¢

    $$\$35.85 \xrightarrow{-40¢} \$35.45 \xrightarrow{-5¢} \$35.40$$

    $35.85 – 48¢

    $$\$35.85 \xrightarrow{-40¢} \$35.45 \xrightarrow{-5¢} \$35.40 \xrightarrow{-3¢} \$35.37$$

-   Use the problem in **tasks 2-3, textbook p. 99,** to discuss ways of subtracting when there are not enough cents to subtract from. The example shown here is for 2(c) and subtracts cents directly from $1. Use mental math techniques for making 100. Give some additional examples.

    $1.25 – 35¢
    Subtract 35¢ from the dollar.
    $1 – 35¢ = 65¢
    Add back in the 25¢
    65¢ + 25¢ = **90¢**

-   Discuss an additional method with 3(b) where $1 is separated from the rest of the dollars, the cents are subtracted from that $1, and then the difference of 10¢ added.
-   We can also do this by subtracting $1 from the first number, then adding back in 10¢.
-   Give a few more examples using other amounts between 90¢ and 99¢. Students can choose the method they are most comfortable with.

    $14.65 – 90¢
    $14.65
    $13.65 $1
    Subtract 90¢ from $1
    $1 – 90¢ = 10¢
    Add to the $13.65
    $13.65 + 10¢ = **13.75**

    $14.65 – 90¢
    $1 = 90¢ + 10¢
    $14.65 – $1 = $13.65
    $13.65 + 10¢ = **$13.75**

    $26.15 – 97¢
    $1 = 97¢ + 3¢
    $26.15 – $1 = $25.15
    $25.15 + 3¢ = **$25.18**

-   Discuss **textbook p. 98**. Sets of money can be subtracted by first subtracting the dollars, and then the cents, using mental math techniques.
-   Discuss **task 4, textbook p. 99**.
-   Have students do the problems in **task 5, textbook p. 99**.

2. Subtract money within $100 using the subtraction algorithm.
   - Discuss the first problem in **task 6, textbook p. 100**.
   - Have students do the rest of the problems in this task.
   - Use **task 7, textbook p. 100,** to remind students how to subtract when renaming occurs over more than one place value. The same techniques can be used in subtracting money.

Activity 5.3b   **More Mental Math**

1. Subtract money from a multiple of $10 using mental math strategies.

   - Write a problem where an amount of money is subtracted from $10, such as $10 – $6.43. Have them first solve this problem using the formal algorithm.

     $10 – $6.43

     $$\begin{array}{r} {}^{9}{}^{9} \\ \cancel{1}\,{}^{1}\cancel{0}\,{}^{1}\cancel{0}\,{}^{1}0 \\ -\quad 6\ 4\ 3 \\ \hline 3\ 5\ 7 \end{array}$$

     $10 – $6.43 = $3.57

   - Tell students that they can also solve this problem mentally. $10 is $9 and $1. They can subtract the dollars from $9, and the cents from $1, using mental math strategies for making 100.

     $10 – $6.43
     $9 $1

     $9 - $6 = $3
     100¢ – 43¢ = 57¢

     $10 – $6.43 = $3.57

   - Ask students for suggestions on how they would subtract $6.43 from $30. They can split $30 into $20 and $10 and subtract $6.43 from $10.
   - Or, they can split $30 into $29 and $1 and subtract the dollars from $29 and the cents from $1.
   - Do some other examples where they are subtracting an amount less than $10 from a multiple of $10.

     $30 – $6.43
     $20 $10

     $10 – $6.43 = $3.57
     $20 + $3.57 = $23.57

     $30 = $29 + $1
     $29 – $6 = $23
     $1 – 43¢ = 57¢
     $23 + 57¢ = $23.57

   - Write a problem where an amount over $10 is being subtracted from a multiple of $10, such as $50 – $26.43 and ask for suggestions on how this can be solved using mental math. They can split $50 into $49 and $1 and subtract the dollars from $49 and the cents from $1.

     $50 – $26.43
     $49 $1

     $49 – $26 = $23
     $1 – 43¢ = 57¢
     $23 + 57¢ = $23.57

- Now write a problem where an amount over $10 is subtracted from $100 and ask for suggestions on how this can be solved using mental math. They can split $100 into $99 and $1.

$100 - $26.43
$99 $1

$99 - $26 = $73
$1 - 43¢ = 57¢
$73 + 57¢ = $73.57

2. Have students do **task 8, textbook p. 100**. They can use mental techniques, or the standard algorithm.

3. Practice.
   - Use the "store cards" created earlier. Divide students into groups and provide each group with a set of store cards. Students lay all the cards face up.
   - One student finds the difference between the amounts on two of the cards and gives them the difference, without letting the others know which two amounts were used. The other students try to determine which two amounts were used. The one who gets the correct answer first is the next one to select two items, find the difference in the amounts, and see if the others can determine which two were used.
   - If you have labeled items in the classroom with prices, this game can be played with the entire class.

Workbook Exercise 49

Activity 5.3c   **Word problems**

1. Solve word problems involving addition of money.
   - Discuss **tasks 9-11, textbook pp. 100-101**.
   - Draw the bar diagrams as you discuss tasks 10 and 11 so students can relate the different parts of the diagrams to the information given in the problem.
   - Provide some other word problems for practice. You can use some of the problems in **Practice 5B, textbook p. 102**.
   - For capable students, include a few more challenging problems so that you can discuss different possible solutions with the class. Let the class work on these problems and ask one student to draw a diagram and show how he or she solved it. See if another student has a different method. Do not simply provide them with a solution. Only use whole numbers of dollars if multiplication or division is involved. For example:
     o One package of cookies and one package of crackers together cost $1.20. Kristi bought 2 packages of cookies and 3 packages of crackers for $3.05. How much does a package of crackers cost? ($0.65)
     o Peter and Paul have $89.60 altogether. If Paul has $32.30, how much more money does Peter have than Paul? ($25)
     o Patsy and Tina have $89.60 altogether. If Patsy has $19.60 more than Tina, how much money does Tina have? ($35)
     o Adrienne has $14.50. Katlin has $3.55 more than Adrienne. Zoe has $6.40 less than Katlin. How much does Zoe have? (11.65)
     o Tom has $16.50 and George has $24.50. How much must George give to Tom so that they have the same amount? ($4)

- Have students use the "store cards" to come up with word problems of their own that the other students can find the answer or see if their classmate's problem makes sense.

Workbook Exercise 50

Activity 5.3d   Practice

1. Use **Practice 5B, textbook pp. 102,** and **Practice 5C, textbook p. 103,** for practice and review.
   - If you call on students to solve the problems, have them diagram the word problems for the rest of the class even if they were able to solve them without a diagram.

2. Allow students to play any of the store games they liked for review.

Workbook Exercise 51

Review

Objectives

- Review previous topics

Suggested number of sessions: 4

	Objectives	Textbook	Workbook	Activities
77 78 79 80	▪ Review	p. 104, Review B	Review 5 Review 6	R.2

Activity R.2   **Review**

1. Have students do **Review B, textbook 104.**
   - You may also want to discuss parts of Review 5 and 6 from the workbook in class.

2. Play any favorite games or do other practice, particularly fact practice for multiplication and division by 6, 7, 8, and 9 and for multiplying and dividing a 3-digit number by a 1-digit number.

Mental Math Worksheets Answer Key

Mental Math 1

1.	3688	17.	2002
2.	8942	18.	8864
3.	8303	19.	5300
4.	6312	20.	5242
5.	5730	21.	3669
6.	8303	22.	4692
7.	7741	23.	2954
8.	9774	24.	6590
9.	3468	25.	3501
10.	6588	26.	2840
11.	4240	27.	2312
12.	3720	28.	6400
13.	9776	29.	2002
14.	8239	30.	1855
15.	1224	31.	9000
16.	7262	32.	4241

Mental Math 2

1.	44	16.	141
2.	440	17.	1480
3.	4400	18.	3450
4.	1251	19.	3457
5.	2510	20.	3500
6.	5100	21.	402
7.	5101	22.	1002
8.	5121	23.	1012
9.	1500	24.	797
10.	1501	25.	8341
11.	2000	26.	9041
12.	2020	27.	9115
13.	2029	28.	9169
14.	130	29.	2027
15.	73	30.	10000

Mental Math 3

1.	55	18.	93
2.	550	19.	2093
3.	5500	20.	30
4.	62	21.	2030
5.	620	22.	80
6.	6200	23.	3370
7.	462	24.	648
8.	4620	25.	1254
9.	4622	26.	61
10.	3462	27.	840
11.	126	28.	54
12.	2450	29.	442
13.	1987	30.	26
14.	1492	31.	342
15.	2458	32.	4492

Mental Math 4

1.	999	16.	500
2.	990	17.	450
3.	910	18.	445
4.	900	19.	945
5.	100	20.	995
6.	901	21.	43
7.	877	22.	329
8.	544	23.	140
9.	211	24.	813
10.	760	25.	970
11.	759	26.	1970
12.	959	27.	1655
13.	300	28.	8418
14.	270	29.	1000
15.	265	30.	1000

Mental Math 5

1.	4	16.	30
2.	25	17.	30
3.	12	18.	12
4.	20	19.	9
5.	50	20.	16
6.	10	21.	0
7.	21	22.	15
8.	45	23.	8
9.	14	24.	24
10.	40	25.	24
11.	20	26.	0
12.	35	27.	27
13.	28	28.	16
14.	18	29.	18
15.	36	30.	32

Mental Math 6

1.	10	16.	8
2.	4	17.	10
3.	8	18.	7
4.	10	19.	3
5.	4	20.	1
6.	4	21.	5
7.	6	22.	5
8.	1	23.	7
9.	0	24.	5
10.	6	25.	5
11.	1	26.	5
12.	9	27.	7
13.	7	28.	0
14.	9	29.	8
15.	6	30.	1

Mental Math 7

1.	7	16.	32
2.	21	17.	3
3.	2	18.	90
4.	3	19.	24
5.	60	20.	1
6.	8	21.	45
7.	35	22.	9
8.	9	23.	0
9.	70	24.	2
10.	36	25.	40
11.	24	26.	10
12.	18	27.	30
13.	4	28.	8
14.	0	29.	28
15.	27	30.	10

Mental Math 8

1.	4500	16.	3200
2.	1200	17.	100
3.	280	18.	2700
4.	1200	19.	400
5.	3500	20.	180
6.	140	21.	2000
7.	1600	22.	150
8.	240	23.	800
9.	360	24.	3000
10.	90	25.	1600
11.	250	26.	2100
12.	4000	27.	120
13.	1800	28.	2400
14.	200	29.	40
15.	4000	30.	5000

Mental Math 9

1.	231		
2.	150 + 20 = 170		
3.	160 + 14 = 174		
4.	160 + 12 = 172		
5.	120 + 15 = 135		
6.	425	16.	320
7.	124	17.	141
8.	165	18.	124
9.	129	19.	138
10.	252	20.	84
11.	46	21.	410
12.	168	22.	196
13.	180	23.	72
14.	142	24.	249
15.	84	25.	135

Mental Math 10

1.	18	16.	6
2.	60	17.	8
3.	36	18.	6
4.	54	19.	1
5.	48	20.	3
6.	12	21.	4
7.	30	22.	7
8.	20	23.	5
9.	42	24.	9
10.	32	25.	7
11.	24	26.	10
12.	0	27.	4
13.	21	28.	7
14.	54	29.	9
15.	42	30.	9

Mental Math 11

1.	42	16.	8
2.	63	17.	6
3.	54	18.	8
4.	56	19.	7
5.	35	20.	4
6.	56	21.	2
7.	42	22.	1
8.	28	23.	3
9.	36	24.	5
10.	35	25.	6
11.	63	26.	7
12.	48	27.	9
13.	49	28.	5
14.	343	29.	9
15.	546	30.	7

Mental Math 12

1.	72	16.	6
2.	40	17.	8
3.	64	18.	9
4.	48	19.	5
5.	40	20.	7
6.	32	21.	4
7.	56	22.	6
8.	64	23.	9
9.	42	24.	8
10.	48	25.	7
11.	56	26.	6
12.	36	27.	8
13.	49	28.	3
14.	344	29.	8
15.	656	30.	2

Mental Math 13

1.	54	16.	6
2.	49	17.	9
3.	81	18.	7
4.	63	19.	9
5.	64	20.	8
6.	45	21.	5
7.	72	22.	6
8.	54	23.	6
9.	63	24.	9
10.	27	25.	7
11.	36	26.	3
12.	36	27.	7
13.	72	28.	9
14.	558	29.	4
15.	189	30.	8

Mental Math 14

1.	72	16.	6
2.	6	17.	8
3.	5	18.	6
4.	63	19.	6
5.	48	20.	7
6.	9	21.	81
7.	42	22.	5
8.	8	23.	64
9.	63	24.	49
10.	72	25.	54
11.	9	26.	9
12.	7	27.	56
13.	7	28.	7
14.	8	29.	9
15.	42	30.	56

Mental Math 16

1.	348	16.	9757
2.	533	17.	8
3.	9	18.	44
4.	742	19.	99
5.	48	20.	168
6.	999	21.	810
7.	2720	22.	1443
8.	8	23.	6400
9.	208	24.	3157
10.	536	25.	540
11.	5600	26.	9
12.	3160	27.	568
13.	4800	28.	4547
14.	8	29.	958
15.	420	30.	3500

Mental Math 15

x	4	9	6	2	7	3	8	5
6	24	54	36	12	42	18	48	30
7	28	63	42	14	49	21	56	35
8	32	72	48	16	56	24	64	40
9	36	81	54	18	63	27	72	45

x	5	7	4	6	2	3	9	8
8	40	56	32	48	16	24	72	64
7	35	49	28	42	14	21	63	56
9	45	63	36	54	18	27	81	72
6	40	42	24	36	12	18	54	48

x	2	7	3	6	4	5	9	8
9	18	63	27	54	36	45	81	72
7	14	49	21	42	28	35	63	56
8	16	56	24	48	32	40	72	64
6	12	42	18	36	24	30	54	48

Textbook Answer Key

Unit 1 - Numbers to 10,000

Part 1: Thousands, Hundreds, Tens and Ones (pp. 6-11)

(a) 349 (b) 2435
(c) five thousand. nine hundred ninety-eight six thousand, twelve
1. (a) 3274
2. (a) 2045 (b) 1307 (c) 4250
3. 800; 4
4. (a) 500 (b) 5000 (c) 50
5. 4; 400 3; 3000
6. 8 - 8000 1 - 100
   3 - 30 7 - 7
7. (a) 4316; 5264
   (b) 2325; 2352
8. (a) US: less 3rd: smaller
   (b) US: less 3rd: smaller
   (c) greater
9. 5073 4973
10. 1000 9999
11. 4123, 3412, 3142, 2431
12. 913, 1703, 1892, 9003
13. 540 405
14. (a) 8720 (b) 3479

Practice 1A (p. 12)

1. (a) 2163 (b) 8008 (c) 3600
   (d) 1376 (e) 4005
2. (a) one thousand, three hundred forty-seven
   (b) five thousand, nine hundred
   (c) seven thousand, fifty-eight
3. (a) 6000 + 300 + 50 + 2
   (b) 4000 + 90 + 1
   (c) 7000 + 4
4. (a) 1205 (b) 3020 (c) 2032
5. (a) 1736 (b) 7504 (c) 90
   (d) 800 (e) 3 (f) 900
6. (a) 3776 (b) 2060

Practice 1B (p. 13)

1. (a) US: less 3rd: smaller
   (b) greater
   (c) greater
   (d) US: less 3rd: smaller
   (e) US: less 3rd: smaller
   (f) US: less 3rd: smaller
2. (a) 7711 (b) 8812
3. (a) 9099 (b) 8445

4. 1260, 1098, 989, 208
5. 350, 3005, 3050, 3500, 5003

Part 2: Number Patterns (pp. 14-16)

6442 is 100 more
6542 is 100 more
6542
6642
(a) 6642; 6742
(b) 9342; 10,342
(c) 6345; 6346
(d) 6372; 6382
1. (a) 3724 (b) 3625
   (c) 3634 (d) 4624
2. (a) 4732 (b) 5731
   (c) 5722 (d) 5632
3. (a) 1708, 1718
   (b) 1978, 2078
   (c) 4678, 5678, 6678, 7678
4. (a) 3100 (b) 3128 (c) 4098
   (d) 3298 (e) 8893 (f) 8093

Practice 1C (p. 17)

1. (a) 800 (b) 8
   (c) 8000 (d) 80
2. 5 stands for 5000
   6 stands for 600
   2 stands for 20
   9 stands for 9
3. (a) 4; 40 (b) 0; 0
4. (a) 2010, 2011, 2012
   (b) 5642, 5652, 5662
   (c) 2100, 2200, 2300
   (d) 7056, 8056, 9056
5. (a) 1000 (b) 2009 (c) 5780
   (d) 5000 (e) 4040
6. (a) 5399 (b) 3520 (c) 2350
   (d) 5160 (e) 5692

Unit 2 - Addition and Subtraction

Part 1: Sum and Difference (pp. 18-21)

(a) 11; 11 (b) 3; 3
1. (a) 13; 13 (b) 3; 3
2. (a) 144 (b) 36
3. (a) 21 (b) 12
   (c) 12 (d) 9
4. 388
5. 316

6. 15
7. 121

Practice 2A (p. 22)

1. (a) 874   (b) 408   (c) 802
2. (a) 1000   (b) 400   (c) 800
3. (a) 480   (b) 564   (c) 155
4. (a) 248   (b) 438   (c) 150
5. 312
6. 611
7. 126
8. 221
9. 78

Practice 2B (p. 23)

1. (a) 1043   (b) 484   (c) 426
2. (a) 908   (b) 494   (c) 1143
3. (a) 430   (b) 123   (c) 218
4. (a) 99   (b) 329   (c) 13
5. $1300
6. 365
7. (a) 1120   (b) 2065
8. (a) 24   (b) 11
9. (a) 653   (b) 1483

Part 2: Adding Ones, Tens, Hundreds and Thousands (pp. 24-27)

1. (a) 4268   (b) 4283
    (c) 4663   (d) 7263
    (e) 4688   (f) 7688
2. 2050
3. 5900
4. 4000
5. (a) 1262   (b) 3654
    (c) 4839   (d) 7542
    (e) 7197   (f) 8362
7. (a) 1520   (b) 8920
    (c) 6258   (d) 8037
    (e) 8091   (f) 7382
9. (a) 6013   (b) 7400
    (c) 8800   (d) 5400

Part 3: Subtracting Ones, Tens, Hundreds and Thousands (pp. 28-33)

1. (a) 6844   (b) 6827
    (c) 6347   (d) 2847
    (e) 6324   (f) 2324
2. 5334
3. 4420
4. 6700
5. (a) 4307   (b) 4328

(c) 6282   (d) 5477
(e) 8821   (f) 2625
7. (a) 7428   (b) 4188
    (c) 3791   (d) 2714
    (e) 5666   (f) 1833
9. (a) 1897   (b) 2879
    (c) 4781   (d) 1097
12. (a) 3608   (b) 2155
    (c) 590   (d) 2926
14. (a) 4578   (b) 6155
    (c) 5128   (d) 684
    (e) 1587   (f) 4279

Practice 2C (p. 34)

1. (a) 9779   (b) 4895   (c) 4251
2. (a) 8960   (b) 8000   (c) 3414
3. (a) 7564   (b) 869   (c) 2564
4. (a) 5334   (b) 4595   (c) 879
5. 2195
6. 815
7. $1487
8. $310
9. 5143
10. $4467

Practice 2D (p. 35)

1. (a) 7180   (b) 6520   (c) 4049
2. (a) 9887   (b) 6903   (c) 4256
3. (a) 9042   (b) 1872   (c) 1687
4. (a) 7703   (b) 2429   (c) 3519
5. 418
6. 1159
7. 768
8. $463
9. (a) $3527   (b) $1473
10. (a) 321   (b) 2129

Part 4: Two-step Word Problems (pp 36-37)
    9
1. 17
2. 301

Practice 2E (p. 38)

1. 3001
2. 1260
3. 235
4. $1267
5. $2628
6. $400
7. 1008
8. $1208

Unit 3 – Multiplication and Division

Part 1: Looking Back (pp. 39-42)

1. 12; 12; 12; 12
2. 7   10   7   4
3. (a) 6   (b) 4
   (c) 2   (d) 0
4. (a) 6   (b) 4
   (c) 2   (d) 0
5. 40
6. 7

Practice 3A (p. 43)

1. (a) 12   (b) 8
   (c) 0   (d) 5
2. (a) 30   (b) 7
   (c) 20   (d) 0
3. (a) 0   (b) 9
   (c) 36   (d) 9
4. 24
5. 6
6. $40
7. $6
8. 60
9. $12
10. 9
11. 8

Part 2: More Word Problems (pp. 44-46)

1. 8
2. 7
3. 30
4. 28

Practice 3B (p. 47)

1. (a) 12   (b) 8
   (c) 14   (d) 8
2. (a) 21   (b) 7
   (c) 30   (d) 4
3. (a) 12   (b) 5
   (c) 32   (d) 7
4. (a) 35   (b) 4
   (c) 20   (d) 6
5. (a) 90   (b) 7
   (c) 27   (d) 9
6. 5
7. $30
8. $80
9. 9 kg
10. (a) 8   (b) 32
11. (a) 40   (b) 70
12. 36

Practice 3C (p. 48)

1. (a) 5   (b) 7
   (c) 18   (d) 7
2. (a) 18   (b) 3
   (c) 35   (d) 8
3. (a) 9   (b) 0
   (c) 24   (d) 5
4. (a) 32   (b) 9
   (c) 0   (d) 7
5. (a) 0   (b) 7
   (c) 24   (d) 0
6. $70
7. 5 kg
8. 14
9. US: 4 quarts 3rd: 4 liters
10. 12
11. 10
12. $27

Part 3: Multiplying Ones, Tens, and Hundreds (p. 49-53)

120   1200
1. (a) 45   (b) 450   (c) 4500
   (d) 45   (e) 450   (f) 4500
6. (a) 162   (b) 48   (c) 111
   (d) 208   (e) 92   (f) 225
   (g) 189   (h) 120   (i) 152
9. (a) 428   (b) 969   (c) 924
   (d) 1860   (e) 902   (f) 702
   (g) 867   (h) 3520   (i) 2180

Practice 3D (p. 54)

1. (a) 180   (b) 240
   (c) 2000   (d) 1000
2. (a) 240   (b) 50
   (c) 4000   (d) 1600
3. (a) 100   (b) 120
   (c) 800   (d) 1500
4. (a) 240   (b) 300
   (c) 1200   (d) 2800
5. (a) 240   (b) 180
   (c) 2800   (d) 2000
6. (a) 96   (b) 288
   (c) 260   (d) 116
7. (a) 98   (b) 172
   (c) 225   (d) 215
8. 240
9. 96
10. 280
11. 228
12. $152

Practice 3E (p. 55)

1. (a) 1200   (b) 936
   (c) 2095   (d) 2200
2. (a) 1802   (b) 1524
   (c) 2500   (d) 1960
3. (a) 3070   (b) 1728
   (c) 3905   (d) 1869
4. (a) 4000   (b) 1012
   (c) 1756   (d) 2780
5. (a) 747   (b) 1805
   (c) 3872   (d) 1408
6. 378
7. $1048
8. 780
9. 1250 g
10. 3400
11. $900

Practice 3F (p. 56)

1. (a) 24   (b) 42
   (c) 80   (d) 72
2. (a) 446   (b) 2108
   (c) 258   (d) 978
3. (a) 756   (b) 3052
   (c) 1860   (d) 852
4. (a) 1448   (b) 315
   (c) 1656   (d) 600
5. (a) 780   (b) 2075
   (c) 2545   (d) 1236
6. 840
7. 1460
8. 525
9. 700 g
10. $360
11. 143

Part 4: Quotient and Remainder (pp. 57-64)

   3   2
6. (a) 0   (b) 1

Part 5: Dividing Hundreds, Tens, and Ones (pp. 61-64)

   200 250 275
3. (a) 24   (b) 20   (c) 18
   (d) 12 R 3   (e) 15   (f) 13 R 2
6. (a) 88   (b) 320   (c) 86 R 3
   (d) 233 R 1   (e) 72 R 2   (f) 35
   (g) 62 R 1   (h) 187   (i) 102 R 1

Practice 3G (p. 65)

1. (a) 41   (b) 19 R 1
   (c) 76   (d) 16
2. (a) 22 R 3   (b) 15
   (c) 12 R 1   (d) 15 R 2
3. (a) 96   (b) 175 R 2
   (c) 59 R 4   (d) 85 R 4
4. (a) 200   (b) 426 R 1
   (c) 82 R 2   (d) 167
5. (a) 149   (b) 225
   (c) 137 R 2   (d) 30 R 3
6. 51 R 1
7. 150 g
8. 105 R 1
9. 18 R 2
10. 143

Practice 3H (p. 66)

1. (a) 100   (b) 21
   (c) 204   (d) 25
2. (a) 111   (b) 10
   (c) 156   (d) 12
3. (a) 1248   (b) 41
   (c) 2500   (d) 102
4. (a) 3455   (b) 67 R 2
   (c) 1821   (d) 166 R 2
5. (a) 2304   (b) 135 R 4
   (c) 3525   (d) 65 R 3
6. 320
7. (a) 104   (b) $312
8. 70
9. $86
10. $17

Review A (p. 67)

1. (a) 1970   (b) 5463   (c) 10,000
2. (a) 3645   (b) 2317   (c) 1
3. (a) 141   (b) 1035   (c) 3156
4. (a) 26   (b) 175   (c) 90 R 1
5. 2720
6. 2616
7. 1940 gal [ℓ]
8. (a) 187 dresses   US: 2 yd left
                     3rd: 2 m left
   (b) $935
9. 176
10. $960

Unit 4 - Multiplication Tables of 6, 7, 8, and 9

Part 2: Multiplying and Dividing by 6 (pp. 70-74)

18   5
1. (a) 24   (b) 30
2. (a) 36   (b) 42
   (c) 48   (d) 56
4. 5   7   8   9
6. (a) 204   (b) 342   (c) 414
   (d) 648   (e) 2832   (f) 5460
8. (a) 16   (b) 14 R 5   (c) 12 R 3
   (d) 57   (e) 118   (f) 102 R 3

Practice 4A (p. 75)

1. (a) 18   (b) 24   (c) 42
2. (a) 3   (b) 4   (c) 7
3. (a) 258   (b) 564   (c) 342
4. (a) 13 R 2   (b) 67 R 3   (c) 93 R 4
5. (a) 6   (b) 6
   (c) 6   (d) 10
6. 84
7. 14
8. $510
9. 32
10. $70
11. $36

Part 3: Multiplying and Dividing by 7 (pp. 76-79)

   (a) $14   (b) $28
   (c) 5   (d) 6
1. (a) 21   (b) 35
2. (a) 42   (b) 49
   (c) 56   (d) 63
3. 14   28   70
5. (a) 42   (b) 49   (c) 63
   (d) 8   (e) 10   (f) 3
6. (a) 392   (b) 441   (c) 497
   (d) 6440   (e) 5628   (f) 1526
7. (a) 10 R 5   (b) 12   (c) 9 R 1
   (d) 13   (e) 14   (f) 11 R 3
8. (a) 15 R 3   (b) 33   (c) 97 R 3
   (d) 104 R 2 (e) 136 R 2 (f) 100 R 5

Practice 4B (p. 80)

1. (a) 28   (b) 42
   (c) 21   (d) 63
2. (a) 4   (b) 6
   (c) 3   (d) 9

3. (a) 280   (b) 4256
   (c) 5600   (d) 6510
4. (a) 13 R 4   (b) 77 R 1
   (c) 102   (d) 115
5. 21 R 3
6. 364
7. 9
8. $182
9. $12
10. $48
11. $208

Practice 4C (p. 81)

1. (a) 36   (b) 56
   (c) 60   (d) 49
2. (a) 6   (b) 7
   (c) 10   (d) 7
3. (a) 469   (b) 0
   (c) 10   (d) 3591
4. (a) 50 R 4   (b) 0
   (c) 1   (d) 121
5. US: 23 in. 3rd: cm
6. $168
7. 14
8. 24
9. 48
10. $235

Part 4: Multiplying and Dividing by 8 (pp. 82-83)

   64   72
1. 6; 10; 12; 32; 64
2. (a) 24   (b) 40   (c) 64
   (d) 32   (e) 56   (f) 72
3. (a) 10   (b) 6   (c) 3
   (d) 9   (e) 7   (f) 5
4. (a) 448   (b) 632   (c) 544
   (d) 3344   (e) 2440   (f) 4960
5. (a) 12 R 2   (b) 14   (c) 100 R 7
   (d) 38 R 1   (e) 83   (f) 120

Practice 4D (p. 84)

1. (a) 24   (b) 48
   (c) 80   (d) 64
2. (a) 3   (b) 7
   (c) 10   (d) 8
3. (a) 344   (b) 776
   (c) 2096   (d) 6992
4. (a) 15   (b) 72 R 3
   (c) 93 R 1   (d) 104
5. (a) 4   (b) 6
   (c) 8   (d) 9

6. 288
7. 144 liters
8. 48 R 6
9. $4
10. $1069

Practice 4E (p. 85)

1. (a) 42   (b) 56
   (c) 80   (d) 72
2. (a) 7   (b) 8
   (c) 6   (d) 9
3. (a) 10 R 3   (b) 8
   (c) 0   (d) 18 R 6
4. (a) 117 R 7   (b) 8
   (c) 0   (d) 145 R 2
5. 24 R 1
6. 24
7. 960
8. $68
9. $9

Part 5: Multiplying and Dividing by 9 (pp. 86-88)

   72 81
1. 9
2. 63 81
3. (a) 2   3   4   5   (b) 2
4. (a) 18   (b) 36   (c) 27
   (d) 72   (e) 81   (f) 63
5. (a) 10   (b) 7   (c) 5
   (d) 6   (e) 8   (f) 9
6. (a) 486   (b) 657   (c) 720
   (d) 1809   (e) 6102   (f) 5481
7. (a) 10 R 7   (b) 12   (c) 9 R 8
   (d) 68 R 8   (e) 100 R 3 (f) 16 R 1

Practice 4F (p. 89)

1. (a) 27   (b) 36
   (c) 45   (d) 81
2. (a) 3   (b) 4
   (c) 5   (d) 9
3. (a) 324   (b) 3600
   (c) 5913   (d) 1782
4. (a) 106   (b) 62 R 5
   (c) 87 R 7   (d) 91 R 4
5. 162
6. 225
7. $16
8. 102
9. 1665 liters

10. 135
11. $18

Practice 4G (p. 90)

1. (a) 54   (b) 70
   (c) 64   (d) 36
2. (a) 9   (b) 10
   (c) 8   (d) 6
3. (a) 552   (b) 9
   (c) 0   (d) 5406
4. (a) 64 R 5   (b) 9
   (c) 0   (d) 107
5. 4
6. 14
7. $252
8. 816
9. 13
10. 280

Unit 5 – Money

Part 1: Dollars and Cents (pp. 91-92)

   35; 25 67; 25
   75; 40 32; 75
   (a) 74; 40; 74.40
   (b) 7; 61; 7.61
2. (a) 125   (b) 1.70
3. (a) 30¢   (b) 195¢   (c) 405¢
4. (a) $0.85   (b) $1.60   (c) $3.45
5. (a) 0.30   (b) 0.45

Practice 5A (p. 93)

1. (a) 20¢   (b) 65¢   (c) 700¢
   (d) 205¢   (e) 560¢   (f) 395¢
2. (a) $0.05   (b) $0.60   (c) $4.00
   (d) $2.10   (e) $8.55   (f) $3.05
3. (a) 70¢   (b) 55¢
   (c) 60¢   (d) 35¢
4. US: (a) $1.50   (b) $0.60   (c) $2.10
   3rd: (a) $1.60   (b) $0.60   (c) $1.80
5. $4.70

Part 2: Addition (pp. 94-97)

   19.75
1. (a) $1.70   (b) $14.85   (c) $38.75
   (d) $3.00   (e) $26.00   (f) $34.00
2. (a) 3.05   (b) $3.30   (c) $6.10
   (d) $17.40   (e) $25.65

3. (a) 29.70; 29.80; 29.80
   (b) 36.65; 37.00; 37.00
   (c) 35.80; 36.20; 36.20
   (d) 34.70; 35.20; 35.20
4. (a) $20.85   (b) $38.00
   (c) $57.20   (d) $39.30
   (e) $60.50   (f) $55.10
5. (a) $56.70   (b) $38.00   (c) $74.30
   (d) $69.20   (e) $61.10   (f) $61.75
6. 9.75
7. 36.55
8. 9.10

Part 3: Subtraction (pp. 98-101)

   31.20
1. (a) $2.40   (b) $8.45
   (c) $35.40   (d) $1.25
   (e) $6.05   (f) $46.45
2. (a) $0.40   (b) $0.70
   (c) $0.90   (d) $0.55
3. (a) $2.40   (b) $13.75   (c) $45.80
   (d) $31.20   (e) $41.75
4. (a) 12.80; 12.20; 12.20
   (b) 27.70; 27.50; 27.50
   (c) 17.20; 16.70; 16.70
5. (a) $35.50   (b) $34.85
   (c) $45.40   (d) $52.80
   (e) $9.70   (f) $27.25
6. (a) $21.70   (b) $25.50
   (c) $56.80   (d) $16.80
   (e) $41.45   (f) $29.90
7. (a) 5785   (b) $57.85
   (c) 3170   (d) $31.70
8. (a) $5.30   (b) $22.80   (c) $41.75
   (d) $26.20   (e) $47.10   (f) $60.55
9. $4.35
10. $5.40
11. $9.50

Practice 5B (p. 102)

1. (a) $39.70   (b) $100.00
   (c) $75.70   (d) $40.30
   (e) $91.65   (f) $91.00
2. (a) $21.35   (b) $36.05
   (c) $21.60   (d) $23.75
   (e) $45.25   (f) $49.15
3. $101.00
4. $13.90
5. $22.40
6. $3.05
7. $25.65
8. $20.50

Practice 5C (p. 103)

1. (a) $41.00   (b) $3.25
2. (a) $30.60   (b) $25.15
3. (a) $100.00   (b) $18.95
4. (a) $63.40   (b) $9.10
5. (a) $99.90   (b) $28.30
6. $26.60
7. $13.05
8. $1.50
9. $27.40
10. $13.35

Review B (p.104)

1. (a) 701   (b) 1110   (c) 5000
2. (a) 702   (b) 609   (c) 909
3. (a) 294   (b) 1428   (c) 3438
4. (a) 16   (b) 14 R 6 (c) 32 R 4
5. $405
6. US: $14   3rd: 14 kg
7. 58
8. 396
9. $13.00
10. 68

Workbook Answer Key

Exercise 1

1. (a) 1306 (b) 2048 (c) 1344
   (d) 4066 (e) 8009
2. (a) 5278 (b) 2050
   (c) 4207 (d) 6035
3. 2151, 4548, 3302, 1712,
   3400, 6009, 4502
4. five thousand, four hundred seventeen
   six thousand, nine hundred forty
   eight thousand, fifty-three
   seven thousand, two hundred nine
   nine thousand, four

Exercise 2

1. (a) 8, 80, 400, 2000
   (b) 7, 40, 400, 6000
   (c) 9, 90, 700, 7000
2. (a) 90   (b) 8
   (c) 50   (d) 700
   (e) 3000 (f) 600   (g) 200
3. (a) 5, 8, 9, 7
   (b) 5000
   (c) 8, 800
   (d) 9, 5
4. (a) 800   (b) 6   (c) 60
   (d) tens (e) 5, 8

Exercise 3

1. (a) 4073 (b) 5001
2. (a) 4082 (b) 3671
3. (a) US: less   3rd: smaller
   (b) US: less   3rd: smaller
   (c) greater
4. (a) 7640, 7604, 7406, 7064
   (b) 8709, 8790, 8907, 8970
5. (a) 932, 923, 392, 329, 239, 293
   (b) 872, 278
6. 8310
7. 2567

Exercise 4

1. (a) 6335 (b) 2316
2. (a) 395   (b) 590
   (c) 4042 (d) 3507
   (e) 1183 (f) 2716
   (g) 1225 (h) 4717
3. (a) 10   (b) 1000
   (c) 1   (d) 100
   (e) 10   (f) 100
   (g) 1000 (h) 1

4. (a) 1   (b) 100
   (c) 1000 (d) 10
   (e) 1   (f) 1000
   (g) 100   (h) 10
5. (a) 3809 (b) 5038
   (c) 2987 (d) 1299
6. (a) 1302 (b) 903
   (c) 4537 (d) 3698
7. 4044 4054 3734 5635
   3634 6634 5633 5632
   3631 5631 6631 2629
   2628 2828 2928

Exercise 5

1. (a) 16 (b) 2
2. +, 14
3. −, 7
4. 154
5. 430
6. 28
7. 125

Exercise 6

1. 134
2. 19
3. 13
4. 9
5. 3 kg
6. 46
7. $135
8. 173 cm
9. 424

Exercise 7

1. (a) 135, 255
   (b) 135   (c) 255
2. (a) 124, 12
   (b) 124   (c) 12
3. (a) 58   (b) 130
4. (a) $1165 (b) $675

Exercise 8

1. 3627 5109
   2780 5293
   3674 5177
   4965 4870
   3824 5707
   5954 6818
   7624 8107
   5591 7408
   9470 8934

2. 4112   7346   1818
    6465   3074   8291
    9937   5713   7179
    VEGETABLES
3. 3872
4. 4178
5. 1820

Exercise 9

1. A. 6661   B. 9192   C. 5215
    D. 3127   E. 7291   F. 9424
    G. 8692   H. 4154   I. 7260
    tent
2. 4921
3. $2000
4. $2110

Exercise 10

1. 9322   6518   7400
    275   3313   8234
    5236   2593   1260
    U
2. 1509
3. $612
4. 1722

Exercise 11

1. 9388   9589   2329
    1516   3497   1129
    8194   8258   3729
    COURTEOUS
2. 8272   2949   1872
    5785   6786   2837
    4726   3859   7683
    US: PINEAPPLE   3rd: JACKFRUIT

Exercise 12

1.

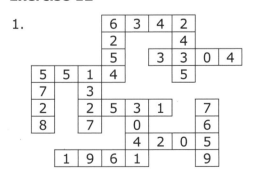

2. 582
3. 1829
4. 927

Exercise 13

1. 2086
2. 1654
3. 865
4. $1408
5. 680
6. $640

Review 1

1. (a) 271   (b) 5702
    (c) 800   (d) 70
2. (a) greater (b) greater
    (c) greater (d) US: less
                     3rd: smaller
    (e) US: less 3rd: smaller
    (f) greater
3. (a) 20   (b) 4   (c) 3
4. (a) 340   (b) 318   (c) 5875
    (d) 515   (e) 870   (f) 8061
5. 210, 450, 300
6. (a) 3034; 3234; 3234
    (b) 1888, 1808; 1808
    (c) 5452, 5460; 5460
    (d) 2804, 2754; 2754
7. 1703
8. 653
9. $2080
10. $470
11. 1894

Exercise 14

1. (a) 24   (b) 15
    (c) 8   (d) 15
2. (a) 9, 12, 15
    (b) 12, 16, 20
    (c) 15, 20, 25
3. (a) 8, 10, 12, 16,
    (b) 12, 15, 18, 24
    (c) 16, 20, 28, 32, 36
    (d) 20, 25, 35, 40
    (e) 40, 50, 70, 80

Exercise 15

1. 27, 27
2. (a) 15, 15   (b) 28, 28
3. (a) 32, 32   (b) 12, 12
    (c) 3, 27, 9, 27

Exercise 16

1. (a) 4, 4   (b) 3, 3
2. 5, 3
3. 6   9, 9   5, 5
    7, 7   9, 9   5, 5
    6, 6   9, 9   8, 8
    2, 2   6, 6   9, 9
4. 4, 5, 4, 2, 3, 9, 9, 8, 7, 8, 9, 4, 8

Exercise 17

1. 30   45
    0   100 36
    50   18   16
    0   21   0   5
    10   32
2. 7, 10, 0, 6, 8, 9, 4, 5, 8, 3, 1, 0

Exercise 18

1. 12
2. 8
3. 6
4. $9
5. 24 m
6. 12 liters

Exercise 19

1. 21
2. $8
3. 5
4. (a) 15, 20   (b) $20   (c) $15
5. (a) 32, 8   (b) $8   (c) $32

Exercise 20

1. 37
2. $9
3. 8
4. 6 m

Exercise 21

1. 12, 120   21, 210
    15, 150   20, 200
    18, 1800   24, 2400
    28, 2800   24, 2400
2.   180   400
    1500   1000   2400
    3000   240   2700
    1200   140   3600

Exercise 22

1. A. 48   R. 84   E. 68
    S. 128   R. 255
    T. 368   U. 168   E. 288
    TREASURE Island
2. (a) 205   (b) 156
3. (a) 129   (b) 248   (c) 355

Exercise 23

1. 74   135   116   344
    185   115   96   228
    195 86   316 490
2. 104, 54, 183, 72, 140, 144, 135, 136,
    130, 177, 200, 280, 400, 388, 224
3. 138
4. 375 cm
5. $240

Exercise 24

1. A. 248   R. 484   E. 1065
    W. 1000   E. 906   T. 748
    V. 912   A. 546   S. 868
    SAVE WATER
2. 435   1540
    1056   990
    4000   1400
    326   2100
    1070   3348
    540   1107
3. $720
4. 416
5. $1925

Exercise 25

1. M. 7 R 1   T. 20   E. 31 R 1
    U. 14 R 1   K. 15   O. 43
    N. 48   R. 41 R 1 Y. 49 R 1
    MONKEY TURKEY

Review 2

1. (a) 942   (b) 4605
    (c) 3004   (d) 6030
2. (a) four thousand, sixty-two
    (b) five thousand, eight hundred eighty
3. 2040, 2030, 2130, 2136, 2186, 1186
4. (a) 2000   (b) 1108
    (c) 3445   (d) 8674
5. (a) 980   (b) 1010
    (c) 978   (d) 2109

6. (a) 309   (b) 2090
   (c) 9009   (d) 4779
7. 2202
8. $168
9. 72
10. 1950
11. 830

Review 3

1. (a)   6   8 10 12 14 16   20
       3   6   12 15 18 21 24 27 30
       4   12 16 20   28 32 36 40
       5 10 15 20 25 30 35   45 50
      10 20 30   50 60 70 80 90 100
   (b) 30 kg, 50 kg, 70 kg, 90 kg, 100 kg
2. 5 x 3 = 15   3 x 5 = 15;
   15 ÷ 3 = 5   15 ÷ 5 = 3
3. (a) 1, 50, 700, 3000
   (b) 3, 70, 0, 7000
4. (a) 15   (b) 9000   (c) 5
   (d) tens   (e) 10
   (f) 106 , 2
5. (a) 12   (b) 32
   (c) 40   (d) 8
6. 201
7. 24
8. $525
9. 520
10. $3150

Exercise 26

1. 41 R 1   16 R 1
   13 R 2   32 R 0
   37 R 1   19 R 2
   26 R 2   19 R 0
2. 24 R 2
3. 14
4. 24

Exercise 27

1. C. 86   E. 86 R 1   M. 82
   O   128   P. 201   R. 314
   S. 204   T. 250   U. 82 R 3
   COMPUTERS
2. $225
3. 37 R 1
4. 81

Exercise 28

1. (a) 6, 12, 16
   (b) 18, 24, 30
   (c) 20, 36, 40
   (d) 25, 40, 50, 55

(e) 50, 60, 90
2. (a) 6, 9, 15, 18, 21, 24, 30
   (b) 8, 12, 16, 24, 28, 36, 40
   (c) 10, 15, 25, 30, 35, 40, 45, 50
   (d) 3, 6, 9, 12, 15, 21, 24, 27, 30
       4, 8, 16, 20, 24, 28, 32, 36, 40
       5, 10, 15, 20, 25, 30, 35, 45, 50
       10, 20, 30, 40, 60, 70, 80, 90, 100
3. (a) 10   (b) 16
   (c) 27   (d) 18
   (e) 60   (f) 16
   (g) 35   (h) 10
   (i) 32   (j) 35
4. 6, 6   10, 10
   8, 8   9, 9
   6, 6   7, 7
   4, 4   9, 9
5. (a) 9   (b) 9
   (c) 3   (d) 8
   (e) 7   (f) 5
   (g) 6   (h) 4
   (i) 6   (j) 3

Exercise 29

1. (a) 30, 30   (b) 36, 36
   (c) 42, 42   (d) 48, 48
   (e) 54, 54   (f) 60, 60
2. 6, 18, 30, 48, 36, 12, 24, 54, 60, 42

Exercise 30

1. (1) 2   (2) 3   (3) 10   (4) 8
   (5) 5   (6) 9   (7) 7   RAINBOW
2. 6   2
   30   7
   18   1
   42   4
   36   10
   54   9
   60   5
   24   3
   12   0

Exercise 31

1.
	2	2	8	
	7			
3	0		5	
1		1	4	4
2	1	0		0
			2	8	8

2.　258　　　450　　　588
　　1836　　2700　　3444
　　4746　　4800　　5538

Exercise 32

1.　T. 8 R 5　　　N. 12 R 3　　G. 14
　　　　P. 10 R 4　　　　　A. 8 R 1
　　O. 16　　　E. 6 R 2　　　N. 9 R 5
　　PENTAGON
2.　15 R 2　　　14 R 0　　　13 R 0
　　133 R 2　　　100 R 5　　　91 R 0
　　82 R 4　　　119 R 5　　　153 R 5

Exercise 33

1.　$270
2.　432
3.　25 R 3
4.　$385
5.　36
6.　30
7.　65 R 4

Exercise 34

1.　21　　　　42　　　　28
　　　　56　　　35
　　　　　　49　　　63
　　70　　14　　　7
2.　(a)　4　　　(b)　6　　　(c)　5
　　(d)　7　　　(e)　9　　　(f)　1
　　(g)　10　　(h)　2
　　(i)　3　　　(j)　8
3.　(1)　14　　(2)　7　　　(3)　28
　　(4)　10　　(5)　56　　(6)　3
　　(7)　49　　(8)　5
　　FLAMINGO

Exercise 35

1.　560　　　378　　　273
　　497　　　434　　　301
　　686　　　245　　　532
2.　672　　　315　　　574
　　4900　　2296　　1015
　　2821　　4578　　3717
　　PRAYING MANTIS

Exercise 36

1.　$7\overline{)80}$ → 11 r3　　$7\overline{)55}$ → 7 r6

　　$7\overline{)69}$ → 9 r6　　$7\overline{)43}$ → 6 r1

$7\overline{)98}$ → 14　　　　$7\overline{)76}$ → 10 r6

$7\overline{)84}$ → 12

2.　E.　13　　　U.　19 R 2　　N.　65
　　G.　133 R 1　P.　110　　　I.　114
　　N.　88 R 3　　S.　102 R 2
　　PENGUINS

Exercise 37

1.　2800 m
2.　91
3.　14 kg
4.　25
5.　625 g
6.　23 m
7.　49

Review 4

1.　(a)　5306　　(b)　8005　　(c)　10,000
2.　(a)　4320　　(b)　8320　　(c)　2645
3.　(a)　US: less　3rd: smaller
　　(b)　US: less　3rd: smaller
　　(c)　US: less　3rd: smaller
4.　(a)　800　　(b)　80　　　(c)　8
5.　(a)　1150　　(b)　1000　　(c)　3661
　　(d)　102 R 6　(e)　200　　(f)　1400
6.　(a)　600　　(b)　400　　(c)　200
7.　136
8.　$23
9.　45
10.　$4800
11.　55

Exercise 38

1.　32　56　24
　　40　64　48
　　72　16　80
2.　3, 5, 8, 2, 6, 4, 9, 7, 10

Exercise 39

1.　(1)　256　　(2)　432　　(3)　400
　　(4)　504　　(5)　704　　(6)　216
　　(7)　288　　(8)　112　　(9)　736
EXCELLENT

2.

3	6	8		5		4	6	4
	4			1	9	9	2	
	2		4	9	6		7	
4	4	0		2	0	3	2	

Exercise 40

1. 7 R 2   8 R 3   6 R 1
    11   9 R 5   12
    4 R 4   9   5 R 3
2. F. 106 R 2   O. 120 R 2   P. 46 R 4
    K. 75 R 2   R. 66   T. 94 R 2
    X. 12 R 7   S. 61   C. 93 R 4
    EXERCISE TO KEEP FIT

Exercise 41

1. 1480 liters
2. 12 kg
3. 112 R 4
4. 1015
5. $102
6. 3
7. 84

Exercise 42

1. 27 45
    90 36
    18 63 54
    81 72
2. 9   10
    3   4
    8   7
    5   6

Exercise 43

1. 126   189   720
    891   792   477
    360   567   648
2. M. 675   L. 954   E. 2376
    I. 4131 N. 4707 A. 5508
    P. 7056 C. 7470 O. 8523
POLICEMAN

Exercise 44

1. 27 ÷ 9 = 3   80 ÷ 9 = 8 R 8
    11 = 99 ÷ 9   90 ÷ 9 = 10
    6 R 5 = 59 ÷ 9   25 ÷ 9 = 2 R 7
2. 103 R 2, 61 R 5, 73, 42 R 3,
    23, 48 R 4, 94 R 6

Exercise 45

1. $504
2. 12
3. US: 38 lb   3rd: kg
4. 56
5. 184

6. 65
7. $13

Exercise 46

1. (a) 30.85   (b) 4.30   (c) 80.07
2. (a) 5.65   (b) 10.08   (c) 17.70
    (d) 90.12   (e) 320.04   (f) 1030.00
3. (a) eighty cents
    (b) one dollar and thirty-six cents
    (c) six dollars and forty-four cents
    (d) seven dollars and ninety-eight
        cents
    (e) twenty-three dollars and twenty
        cents
    (f) ten dollars and five cents
    (g) forty-four dollars and fifty-five
        cents
    (h) four hundred twelve dollars
    (i) three thousand, seven hundred
        nine dollars

Exercise 47

1. (a) 11.90, 11.95
    (b) 9.85, 10.25
    (c) 34.35, 35.10
    (d) 66.35, 67.20
2. (a) $31.30 (b) $35.10
    (c) $69.15 (d) $53.40
3. (a) 1000; $10.00
    (b) 3115; $31.15
    (c) 9485; $94.85
    (d) 10,000; $100.00
4. A. $4.95   E. $16.35   G. $17.60
    I. $80.29   L. $93.73   N. $85.20
    R. $43.85   S. $53.14   T. $73.90
    TRIANGLES

Exercise 48

1. (a) 11.90   (b) 5.90   (c) 20.55
    (d) 13.85   (e) 4.90   (f) 41.40
2. $172.45
3. $160.88
4. $179.50

Exercise 49

1. (a) 2.50, 2.45
    (b) 2.35, 1.55
    (c) 12.00, 11.40
    (d) 17.05, 16.60
2. (a) $5.15   (b) $4.05

(c) $53.60 (d) $53.55
3. (a) 5250; $52.50
   (b) 2525; $25.25
   (c) 4520; $45.20
   (d) 3515; $35.15
4. $37.20 $25.50 $16.15
   $63.45 $16.55 $7.01
   $35.95 $15.85 $9.90
   BADMINTON

Exercise 50

1. (a) $2.25   (b) $1.35   (c) $1.00
   (d) $25.45 (e) $2.10
2. $43.35
3. $45.05
4. $22.05

Exercise 51

1. $15.55
2. $5.00
3. $0.60
4. $6.45

Review 5

1. (a) $200   (b) B
2. (a) five thousand, seven
   (b) one thousand, forty-three
   (c) nine thousand, five hundred sixty
3. 5000
4. 800
5. 4

6. 2; 200
7. 3263; 2030
8. (a) 6553   (b) 3944
   (c) 9107   (d) 4590
9. 450, 18, 9, 36, 288
10. 350
11. 1050 kg
12. 350
13. 114
14. $750

Review 6

1. (a) 4070   (b) 1400
   (c) 6019   (d) 4900
2. (a) 900   (b) 598   (c) 671
3. (a) 2638   (b) 2754
   (c) 6156   (d) 48 R 8
4. (a) 74   (b) 8
5. $7
6. 44 kg
7. 1901
8. US: 262 lb   3rd: 262 kg
9. 21 R 3
10. 75 g
11. $218